The

COAST GUARD RESCUE

of the

SeaBreeze

off the OUTER BANKS

◇◇◇◇◇◇◇◇◇◇◇◇◇◇◇◇◇◇◇◇◇◇◇◇◇◇◇◇◇◇◇◇◇

On the Wings of Angels

REAR ADMIRAL CARLTON MOORE USCGR (RET)

THE
History
PRESS

Published by The History Press
Charleston, SC
www.historypress.com

Copyright © 2021 by Carlton Moore
All rights reserved

Front cover: Artwork by Rick Farrell.
Back cover: Photograph courtesy of Steve Bonn.

First published 2021

Manufactured in the United States

ISBN 9781467147040

Library of Congress Control Number 2021931016

To the men and women of the United States Coast Guard.
You are a special breed.
You do noble things in dangerous places so that others may live.
Semper Paratus!

We should pray to the angels, for they are given to us as guardians.
—Saint Ambrose

CONTENTS

PREFACE

This book is about a Coast Guard search and rescue mission. At the outset, it should be said that discussing one particular mission of the Coast Guard is somewhat problematic. First, and most importantly, the Coast Guard is in the rescue business. It is the expectation of the public that the Coast Guard will do whatever it can to collectively preserve life at sea. However, the Coast Guard has eleven statutory missions. Search and rescue is the one mission that the public knows well and the one that seems to receive the most media attention. Other mission areas, such as ports, waterway and coastal security, drug interdiction, aids to navigation, living marine resources, marine safety, defense readiness, migrant interdiction, marine environmental protection, ice operations, and laws and treaties enforcement are all equal siblings within the Coast Guard family but receive much less print.

There were extraordinary things done during the response to the explosion and fire on the *Deepwater Horizon* drilling rig in the Gulf of Mexico. Of the hundreds of Coast Guard men and women who responded to this incident and spent endless hours on response efforts, most remain nameless.

Coast Guard presence in both the Arctic and the Antarctic is not well known. Few realize that the Coast Guard has the only polar icebreaking capability in the U.S. fleet, and few Americans know the importance of Coast Guard Cutters *Polar Star* and *Healy*. Ice operations also include keeping shipping lanes open on the Great Lakes and coastal harbors to facilitate safe navigation and continuous flow of commerce.

The interdiction and capture of drug runners who bring cocaine and other contraband to our shores receive press when hauls are newsworthy. This important mission, like search and rescue, is 24/7/365 and requires close coordination with other services, federal law enforcement agencies and nations. It may be a Navy gray-hull flying the Coast Guard ensign (flag) with a small Coast Guard law enforcement detachment on board that makes the bust. But this is what the public expects, and many successful operations often go without fanfare.

A huge spectrum of responsibilities encompasses the aids to navigation and marine safety missions. It involves vessel inspection and the licensing of personnel operating ships in U.S. waters. Virtually every American who has ventured out on the water in a boat knows that the lifejackets must be "Coast Guard approved."

The aids to navigation mission includes the design, placement and maintenance of nearly all U.S. buoys, lights and day markers. The Coast Guard publishes a continuous series of Notices to Mariners, which are designed to inform seafarers and enhance safety afloat.

The port, waterways and coastal security mission has been significantly beefed up to support Homeland Security objectives, from checking a United States–bound vessel's cargo manifest overseas to enforcing new, stringent port safety and security protocols at home. Most of the men and women in this mission remain nameless, too, but they are doing what the public expects, and doing it well.

Defense readiness means overseas deployments, usually in support of joint missions. Since its establishment in 2002, in support of Operation Iraqi Freedom, Patrol Forces South West Asia has played a key role in maritime interception operations, maritime infrastructure protection and maritime security operations in the Arabian Gulf. At the height of these operations, over one thousand Coast Guard personnel were deployed to the Arabian Gulf. In 2004, the Coast Guard lost one of its own, Petty Officer Nathan Bruckenthal, in support of this mission.

In 2002, Coast Guard forces arrived at Guantanamo Bay, Cuba, to provide waterside security, sleeping in tents and showering from a garden hose. Although conditions have improved significantly, Coast Guard forces remain deployed to support this mission.

Historically, the Coast Guard has been involved in every major U.S. conflict. During World War II, the Coast Guard swelled to over 200,000; of these, over 1,900 made the ultimate sacrifice in service to the nation. So, I salute those men and women of the Coast Guard who devote their careers to service in other mission areas. You are dedicated to the service of the nation. You do very important work for the Coast Guard. You deserve equal time—at another time.

The second reason that singling out a particular rescue is problematic is the simple fact that Coast Guard personnel routinely conduct incredibly heroic rescues from Alaska to Florida, Puerto Rico, Hawaii and Guam, which receive little attention outside of local press. Saving the life of a local Alaskan fisherman rarely makes for national news coverage even if it involves the most dangerous of circumstances to the crew of the Coast Guard boat or helicopter sent to save him.

Sadly, not all rescues end in "success." There are many instances in which search and rescue turns into search and recovery. But that doesn't lessen the danger that faces a boat crew or air crew doing their very best to bring people to safety. I suppose there is a public perception that a successful rescue means "bringing them home alive," which is very different from a successful operation in launching a response when the odds are against you, but you go out anyway. These heroic Coast Guard operations receive little, if any, press other than to mention the loss of life.

Some rescue operations stand out because they present formidable challenges to the crew and their equipment. The 1990 *Alaskan Monarch* rescue in the Bering Sea was one of these. After flying over 650 miles from Coast Guard Air Station Kodiak in an unrelenting snowstorm, Lieutenant Laura Guth and her helicopter flight crew arrived on the scene to see the *Alaskan Monarch* about to founder on the rocks. After several unsuccessful attempts to get a messenger line from Coast Guard Cutter *Storis*, what started out as a vessel assist operation quickly turned into a helicopter rescue operation. After hoisting most of the vessel's crew, they watched from above as a wave of brash ice engulfed the cargo deck, sweeping the captain and the chief engineer overboard and into the surf zone, which was also choked with ice. LCDR Guth chose to stay on scene, burn increasingly limited fuel and extract both from the grinding ice sheets. Any other decision would have resulted in an entirely different and tragic outcome.

Some incredible rescues catch the attention of Hollywood. Such was the case of Coast Guard Cutter *Tamaroa*, under the command of Commander Larry Brudnicki, in a book titled *The Perfect Storm* by Sebastian Junger and a film by the same name. One citation of the several crew members who were awarded for their heroic action best captures the danger that was posed to the ship and its crew.

Lieutenant FURTNEY is cited for heroism on 30 October 1991 while serving as a member of the rescue team on board CGC TAMAROA during the rescue of three people from the S/V SATORI and four survivors from an Air National Guard (ANG) H-60 helicopter in what became known as The Perfect Storm. The ANG H-60 was forced to ditch because it could not refuel from a C-130 tanker due to the violent turbulence caused by the worst weather in more than 100 years. When a USCG H-3F helicopter could not hoist the ANG crew because the force of the wind was so strong the basket did not go down to the water but went almost straight back into the tail rotor, the TAMAROA became their only hope. As the seas towered above the bridge of the TAMAROA and weather buoys reported wave heights of 100 feet, Lieutenant FURTNEY was exposed to great personal risk as he demonstrated exceptional ship handling expertise for two hours by completing a shipboard pickup of four of the crewmembers of the ANG H-60. By turning beam to the seas and using their power, the TAMAROA was able to approach the ANG crew, but at a cost of taking 55-degree rolls. For the next 36 hours, Lieutenant FURTNEY coordinated the search and rescue effort to locate the final crewmember of the ANG H-60. Assuming tactical control of ten aircraft, he masterfully planned and directed their effort to complete an extensive search and rescue operation, which covered more than 60,000 square miles of ocean. The survivors of the ANG H-60 would certainly have died if Lieutenant FURTNEY had not demonstrated exceptional devotion to duty, supervised the personnel in his department who were stretched to limits of human endurance, and operated with little rest for a 72-hour period during the worst storm of the century. His courage and devotion to duty are most heartily commended and are in keeping with the highest traditions of the United States Coast Guard.

Some rescues naturally overshadow others because of their immense scale. The Coast Guard's responses to the devastating hurricanes of 2017 showed that the service can effectively respond to large-scale catastrophes, saving thousands of lives in the direst of circumstances. During their response to Hurricane Harvey, for example, Coast Guard men and women rescued 11,022 people and 1,384 pets.

Earlier, in 2005, the American public witnessed the immediate surge of helicopters and crews from every Coast Guard district in the United States in response to Hurricane Katrina. The media covered these spectacular rescue operations, which lasted several days. Hot-seat helicopters dropped food and water outbound and returned with people who were in distress. Hurricane

Katrina operations demonstrated—more than at any other operation—the critical importance of the standardization of aviation practices and procedures. Aircrews from across the nation, some of whom were meeting for the first time, formed mixed aircrews, performed flawlessly and saved thousands of lives. Altogether, 12,535 people were hoisted from rooftops, balconies or, in many cases, attics, where the Coast Guard air crews opened roofs with hand axes they had hastily purchased from Home Depot.

However, of equal importance during the response to Hurricane Katrina was the little publicized flotilla of Coast Guard and Coast Guard Auxiliary vessels that were performing miracles on the water. Thirteen cutters and fifty-six smaller vessels helped bring people to safety. Aids to Navigation Teams (ANT) brought another thirty small craft to the effort. Deck barges were converted into floating islands on the Mississippi River to bring stranded residents to safe ground. Coast Guard surface units encountered roving gangs armed with weapons—one Coast Guard Station was even overrun and looted—but they still managed to evacuate approximately 6,600 displaced residents. For the entire response operation, the Coast Guard saved more than 33,500 people, including the evacuation of 9,409 medical patients to safety. The Katrina operation involved a multitude of agencies at all levels of government as well as incredible support from sister services. It was a joint response and a truly collective effort.

Lastly, a rescue may be a singular event, but it involves many people. I was impressed by a statement by LCDR William Sasser, an H-65 helicopter pilot who was credited with 160 rescues during the Hurricane Katrina response. He gave specific credit to the Coast Guardsmen who worked

Petty Officer Second Class Bobby Nash. *U.S. Coast Guard photograph.*

behind the scenes and were so critically important to the mission. "Behind every [air] crew of four, there were 400 [Coast Guard] people pushing the plane forward. This was a complete team effort, and there are guys equally deserving of recognition that never got airborne."[1]

The sea can be unpredictable and terribly unforgiving. Those who wear the Coast Guard uniform and leave the safety of shore in the direst of circumstances know very well the risk they are taking to save the life of another. Some do not return. In the past five decades, ninety members of the Coast Guard aviation community have launched on missions and not returned. Another thirteen Coast Guard Auxiliary members have perished during search operations. A Coast Guard officer, my friend LTJG Carl Johnson, died in a charter helicopter crash while surveying an oil spill near San Francisco Bay. During the same period, twenty-two Coast Guardsmen lost their lives in the line of duty in small boat incidents. Their stories may never be told, but it is important to know that these men and women possessed the same Coast Guard DNA that makes heroes out of regular people.

I have included herein a discussion about the Coast Guard culture, especially as it relates to rescue operations. Readers cannot fully understand that part of the Coast Guard DNA without knowing how these heroes handle (not well) aggrandizement, recognition and award. This curious personality trait is nearly uniform throughout the service, and it begins at the doorstep when entering Coast Guard service. Even though the pilot and copilot of the *SeaBreeze* rescue earned their "wings" in other services, neither of them use *hero* as part of their lexicon.

Like all other military services, the Coast Guard has its requisite share of abbreviations and acronyms, many of which are foreign to the civilian ear. The reader will find several within. Search and rescue (SAR), on-scene commander (OSC) and Rescue Coordination Center (RCC) are just a few. Speeds and distances are given in knots (KT) and nautical miles (NM). Times are given using the twenty-four-hour clock, sometimes referred to as "military time." The United States is in the minority, globally, in the continued use of the twelve-hour ante meridiem (a.m.) and post meridiem (p.m.) method of timekeeping. Herein, 0800 is 8:00 a.m., 1300 is 1:00 p.m., and 1830 is 6:30 p.m. Oddly, in the sea services, 1300 is spoken as "thirteen hundred," while the Army and Air Force strive to eliminate any confusion by calling it "thirteen hundred hours." A glossary of terms has been added to help decode some of these acronyms and abbreviations. Rank and ratings are most often abbreviated, e.g., Lieutenant Junior

Grade is LTJG. Others will be fully identified as we meet them and then shortened for expediency.

Early in the research phase of this project, I enlisted the help of a retired Navy meteorologist to decipher the foreign language of weather forecasting. After much thought, I decided to leave these reports intact with only some translation, believing that the interested reader will wade through them, as I did, to understand just how bad the weather was. Also, it will give insight into the complexity of this science and the depth of knowledge and understanding of weather critical to both the mariner and the aviator.

As we will find out in a later chapter, *M/V Sea Breeze I* is the official name of the ship in this story. Its International Maritime Organization registry number is 5113230. In various pieces of literature and brochures, it is often referred to as SS *SEA BREEZE I*, *SeaBreeze I* or simply *SeaBreeze*. At different times, it had both of the later names prominently displayed on its bow. Historically, it had several other names, and at one point in its service life, it was affectionately known as the Big Red Boat. In an effort to keep it simple, we will call it *SeaBreeze*.

But first, it is important to understand the evolution of the Coast Guard from its predecessor services charged with the saving of life at sea to the preeminent air-sea rescue service of today.

1

IN THE BEGINNING

O n May 29, 1790, Rhode Island became the thirteenth state to ratify the U.S. Constitution. All thirteen states shared one common feature, the Atlantic Seaboard or, in the case of Pennsylvania, waterway access to the sea. Commerce was conducted primarily by sea and so was smuggling. In the nation's infancy, there was a clear need to enforce tariff laws, a main source of federal income, and prevent smuggling. On August 4, 1790, President George Washington signed the Tariff Act, which authorized the Secretary of the Department of the Treasury Alexander Hamilton to construct ten vessels to address smuggling and enforce trade laws on U.S. territorial waters. These vessels were first known as Revenue Cutters, then the fleet of the Revenue Marine and, finally, the Revenue Cutter Service. It would be another eight years before Congress would establish the Navy Department, and for a time, the Revenue Marine was the nation's only armed service afloat. As the nation grew, so did the service and its responsibilities.

A year earlier, Congress had directed the Department of the Treasury to establish the U.S. Life-Saving Service to render assistance to sailors, passengers and cargo of distressed vessels off the shores of the United States. Also in 1789, Congress authorized the creation of the United States Lighthouse Establishment, again within the Department of the Treasury. All locally operated lighthouses were transferred to and funded by the Department. From 1852 to 1910, it was known as the Lighthouse Board, later becoming the Bureau of Lighthouses or the Lighthouse Service.

Each of these nascent services would have a history rich in saving lives at sea and performing rescues in the face of unimaginable challenges.

Revenue Cutter Service

The U.S. Revenue Cutter *Bear* was originally built as a whaler and sealer to operate in the northern latitudes. Its hull was reinforced for sailing in "light" ice. The U.S. Navy acquired it for the Greely Arctic rescue mission in 1884. A year later, it was turned over to the Department of the Treasury and the Revenue Cutter Service. In the ensuing four decades of service, it plied the waters of Alaska and the Arctic Ocean. For nine years, it would sail under the command of "Hell Roaring" Mike Healy, the first African American to command a U.S. government vessel.

Not the least of Healy's accomplishments was the importation of reindeer from Siberia to provide food for the Native Alaskans, who were never free from the threat of famine. As Healy reasoned it, the reindeer would also be an excellent source of clothing and transportation. The wisdom of this measure was dramatically proved a few years later during the famous overland trek to save marooned whalers near Point Barrow, Alaska.

Of all the *Bear*'s exploits, none captured the public's imagination more than its Overland Rescue of 1897. It was the fall of that year when Captain Francis Tuttle, the *Bear*'s new commander, learned that eight whaling vessels and their crews, totaling about 275 men, were trapped in the ice pack off remote Point Barrow, Alaska. The *Bear* had only recently returned from its patrol duties, but at the order of the secretary of the treasury, it prepared to go to the rescue. This was the first time that an Arctic voyage was attempted during the winter season.

By December 14, 1897, it was clear that the *Bear* had gone as far north as it could go. Approximately eighty-five miles off Cape Nome, the ice was so thick that it was forced to turn back. However, before it returned, the

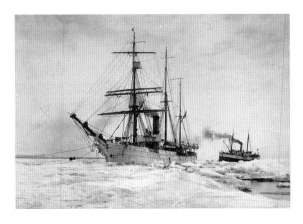

Revenue Cutter *Bear*. *U.S. Coast Guard photograph.*

Bear landed an overland party on Nelson Island, near Cape Vancouver. The group consisted of First Lieutenant D.H. Jarvis, Second Lieutenant B.P. Bertholf and Surgeon S.J. Call, all from the Revenue Cutter Service. Equipped with dog teams, sleds and guides, Jarvis and his companions set out for Point Barrow. Before them lay a 1,600-mile journey through frozen, trackless wilderness. But the "Overland Expedition for the Relief of the Whalers in the Arctic Ocean" became one of the greatest rescue stories of the north.

During the exhausting journey, Jarvis and Call purchased a herd of nearly 450 reindeer. Driving the herd ahead of them in the face of icy winds, the party reached Point Barrow about three and a half months after being put ashore by the *Bear*. To the despairing whalers, the arrival of the relief party was nothing short of a miracle. Captain Healy's foresight of introducing reindeer to Alaska had paid off.[2]

U.S. Life-Saving Service

In the eighteenth and nineteenth centuries, large sections of the United States' Eastern Seaboard were sparsely populated. The crew of any ship running aground could expect very little, if any, help. In a storm, any ship stranded on the sandbars usually went to pieces within a few hours. Few people could survive a three-hundred-yard swim in forty-degree-Fahrenheit storm-tossed surf. Even if a few sailors somehow managed to reach the beach in the winter, they stood a good chance of perishing from exposure on the largely uninhabited shore. The concept of assistance to shipwrecked mariners from shore-based stations began with volunteer lifesaving services. Following a series of tragic shipwrecks that claimed hundreds of lives, the U.S. Life-Saving Service changed to a full-time establishment in 1878.

The service's boats were either seven-hundred or one-thousand-pound, self-bailing, self-righting surfboats pulled by six surfmen with twelve- to eighteen-foot oars or two- to four-ton lifeboats. The surfboats could be pulled on carts by crewmen or horses to a site near a wreck and then launched into the surf. The lifeboats, following a design that originated in England, could be fitted with sails for work farther offshore and were used in very heavy weather. At first, some crews viewed the lifeboats with skepticism because of their great weight and bulk. The skepticism soon changed, and crews began

U.S. Coast Guard photograph.

to regard them as "something almost supernatural," as they enabled them to provide assistance "when the most powerful tugs and steam-craft refused to go out of the harbor."

When a ship wrecked close to shore and the seas were too rough for boats, the service could then use another method to reach the stranded mariners by stringing a strong hawser (line) from the shore to the ship. To propel a messenger line to the ship, a cannon-like gun called the Lyle gun was used. This shot a projectile up to six hundred yards. The projectile carried the small messenger line to the shipwrecked sailors, who were then able to pull out the heavier hawser. With the hawser securely attached to both the vessel and the shore, a breeches buoy and pulley system was used to carry sailors over the surf to safety.[3]

According to statistics compiled by the U.S. Life-Saving Service Heritage Association, over the service's official life of forty-four years and before becoming part of the U.S. Coast Guard in 1915, the U.S. Life-Saving Service was credited with saving over 178,000 persons in peril on the water.

U.S. Life Saving Service Station No. 13, which was located at Kill Devil Hills, North Carolina, is part of this story.

U.S. Lighthouse Service

Statistics of rescues performed by members of the U.S. Lighthouse Service and its predecessors are difficult to obtain. However, reports of especially heroic events are indicative of the important contribution that lighthouse keepers played in saving the lives of mariners who were in distress on our shores. Recently, the Coast Guard recognized the importance of the contributions of just one lighthouse keeper, Kate Moore.

Kathleen "Kate" Moore devoted her entire life to those at sea as the keeper of the Black Rock Harbor Light on Fayerweather Island, a small seaside community south of Bridgeport, Connecticut. Credited with saving over twenty-one lives, Keeper Moore slept in her work clothes while facing the window to make sure her light stayed burning. At a ceremony to honor Kate's service, Vice Admiral Sally Brice-O'Hara stated, "She proved that women performed with distinction—whether the job at hand was harrowing or dutifully and diligently routine."[4]

Coast Guard Cutter *Kathleen Moore*, a sentinel-class vessel that entered service in 2014. *U.S. Coast Guard photograph.*

Keeper Moore first stood the watch at the age of twelve, when her father, the light tender, suffered a shipboard injury that prevented him from going to sea. As Kate grew older, her father's health worsened. She took on most of the duties herself but was not officially appointed as head keeper until 1871. She served at the station for an astounding seventy-two years; she continually braved the harsh storms of Long Island Sound to save those in peril. As keeper, her light was literally the difference between a successful journey and catastrophe for the more than two hundred vessels that sailed the sound nightly. On one particular night, Kate heard cries of distress coming from the harbor. She went out in her rowboat with her brother and cousin searching for the sailor, and after an hour's search, they found two men clinging to a capsized boat.

In her later years, Keeper Moore was interviewed by a reporter who asked her about the dangers she encountered at Black Rock Harbor. "You see, I had done all this for so many years, and I knew no other life, so I was sort of fitted for it," she replied.

On May 10, 2014, Coast Guard Cutter *Kathleen Moore* was commissioned to be home-ported in Key West, Florida. It is one of the new 154-foot sentinel-class cutters named for enlisted Coast Guard heroes.

Standing the watch and tending the lights offshore could be dangerous, and lives were lost in the line of duty. In 1934, the *Nantucket Lightship* was sunk, claiming the lives of seven crew members. While on station in dense fog at Nantucket Shoals Station, the lightship was struck by the RMS *Olympic*, a sister ship of the RMS *Titanic*, and was cut in two and sank almost immediately.[5]

THE U.S. COAST GUARD received its present name in 1915 under an act of Congress that merged the Revenue Cutter Service with the U.S. Life-Saving Service. Legislation creating this "new" Coast Guard expressly stated that it "shall constitute a part of the military forces of the United States," thereby codifying the service's long history of defending the country alongside the nation's other armed services. The Coast Guard began maintaining the country's aids to maritime navigation, including lighthouses, when President Franklin Roosevelt ordered the transfer of the Lighthouse Service to the Coast Guard in 1939. In 1946, Congress permanently transferred the Commerce Department's Bureau of Marine Inspection and Navigation to the Coast Guard, which placed Merchant Marine licensing and merchant vessel safety under its purview. The nation then had a single federal maritime agency dedicated to saving life at sea and enforcing the nation's maritime laws.

The Coast Guard is one of the oldest organizations of the federal government, and until Congress established the Navy Department in 1798, its revenue cutters served as the nation's only armed force afloat. The Coast Guard has protected the nation throughout its long history and has served proudly in the nation's armed conflicts. The Coast Guard's national defense responsibilities remain one of its most important functions even today. In times of peace, it operates as part of the Department of Homeland Security, serving as the nation's frontline agency for enforcing the nation's laws at sea, protecting the marine environment and the nation's vast coastline and ports and saving lives. In times of war, or at the direction of the President, the Coast Guard serves as part of the Navy Department.

Each day, more than forty-three thousand active-duty Coast Guard men and women, over eight thousand reservists and thirty thousand auxiliarists provide services over 3.4 million square miles of exclusive economic zones.

In a single year, the Coast Guard

- Responded to 19,790 search and rescue cases, saved 3,560 lives and more than $77 million in property.
- Removed 107 metric tons of cocaine bound toward the United States via the transit zone.
- Interdicted nearly 3,000 undocumented migrants attempting to illegally enter the United States.
- Conducted over 6,000 fisheries conservation boardings.
- Investigated and responded to over 3,300 pollution incidents.
- Verified more than 70,000 transportation worker identification credentials.
- Screened over 436,000 vessels, including over 117,000 commercial vessels, and 29.5 million crew members and passengers.
- Conducted 919 escorts and patrols to support 190 domestic U.S. military cargo out-loads.
- Conducted 25,500 container inspections, 5,000 facility safety and marine pollution–related inspections and 1,195 cargo transfer monitors to ensure the safety and environmental stewardship of the maritime domain.

- Conducted 1,424 boardings of high-interest vessels designated as posing a greater-than-normal risk to the United States.
- Conducted over 3,700 safety and security exams on vessels operating on the U.S. Outer Continental Shelf.
- Conducted over 11,600 annual inspections on U.S. flag vessels.
- Conducted 4,603 investigations for reportable marine casualties involving commercial vessels.
- Conducted over 49,000 recreational vessel boardings, issued over 12,000 citations and visited 1,150 recreational boat manufacturers in conjunction with state efforts to provide education and ensure compliance with federal regulations.
- Continued the deployment of 6 patrol boats and 400 personnel to protect Iraqi critical maritime oil infrastructure and train Iraqi naval forces.[6]

2

WINGS OVER WATER…AND PIGEONS, TOO

O n April 1, 1916, Second Lieutenant Charles E. Sugden and Third Lieutenant Elmer F. Stone of the Coast Guard received orders to attend aviation training at Pensacola Naval Air Station. This date is considered to be the "birthday" of Coast Guard Aviation. The Naval Appropriation Act of 1916 provided the authorization but not the funding for ten Coast Guard Air Stations to be located along the coasts of the Atlantic and Pacific Oceans, the Great Lakes and the Gulf of Mexico. In March 1920, the first Coast Guard Air Station was opened at Morehead City, North Carolina, with six Curtiss HS-2L flying boats that had been *borrowed* from the U.S. Navy. But the Air Station was closed after fifteen months due to lack of funds. Although the Coast Guard was authorized to build and equip ten Air Stations in 1919, it was not until 1924 that the $13 million was appropriated for their funding.

In 1932, Congress authorized funds for the Coast Guard to design aircraft that met the service's needs. Still, in the early years, many of the aircraft were "interservice transfers," which is code for hand-me-downs. This would include bombers. After World War II, the Coast Guard "acquired" the well-known B-17 Flying Fortress. They were used for search and rescue and other missions. They strapped a boat to the belly of the aircraft and could drop the one-and-a-half-ton boat, with three huge parachutes, to those in distress at sea.

Over time, the Coast Guard would experiment with other means to enhance its ability to carry out missions from the air. Lighter-than-air craft,

U.S. Coast Guard photograph.

such as dirigibles and blimps, were given serious study but never entered the Coast Guard's inventory.

The use of pigeons for search and rescue even made it all the way to operational Coast Guard testing. During the 1940s, pigeons in a Tufts University laboratory had demonstrated an exceptional ability to pick out certain shapes and colors in exchange for food. In the late 1970s and early 1980s, the U.S. Coast Guard decided the same abilities could be useful while searching for men and equipment in open water. Navy scientist Jim Simmons, PhD, used conditioning to train pigeons to conduct search and rescue missions from Coast Guard helicopters. These experiments, called Project Sea Hunt, used three pigeons in a small observation bubble on the underside of a helicopter. The birds were faced 120 degrees from one another so that they covered the entire 360 degrees under the aircraft. The pigeons were trained to recognize objects floating in the water and communicate with the helicopter pilots by pecking a key that would help guide the pilots to the targets.

The pigeons were 93 percent accurate when locating objects floating at sea. In comparison, human flight crews were accurate 38 percent of the time. When combined with human searchers, the pigeons' success rate was nearly perfect. Unlike humans, however, the pigeons did not get bored, as Simmons had trained them to respond even when there were hours between sightings. Eventually, the Coast Guard recognized the value of Simmons's pigeons and called this project "the best daylight search system" that had yet developed. The project, however, was plagued by problems, as two helicopters crashed on separate occasions, either destroying or damaging the pigeon system (pigeons). The project, unfortunately, never got out of the testing phase and was ended in 1983 due to federal budget cuts. Though innovative in theory, the project ultimately proved to be impractical. In the end, the birds never got a chance to save any lives.[7]

U.S. Coast Guard poster.

Air-cushion vehicles were tested for use in search and rescue, aids to navigation, law enforcement, marine safety and logistics. Two of the vessels were stationed in San Francisco, and the other was posted to Alaska. The vehicles were eventually transferred to the Great Lakes. One hovercraft, CG-38103, sank in an accident. The remaining two hovercraft were transferred to the Army in 1975.[8]

On September 30, 2016, the Coast Guard issued a request for information as part of its ongoing market research into small unmanned aircraft systems that could be deployed from its national security cutter fleet. The Coast Guard is interested in an unmanned aircraft system (UAS) that can remain on station for extended periods, expand maritime domain awareness and disseminate actionable intelligence on maritime hazards and threats. Building on developmental work by the other uniformed services and federal agencies, the Coast Guard is considering the UAS to meet both cutter-based and land-based requirements.[9]

From the flying boat to the HU-16 Albatross, the Coast Guard had water landing capability. The HU-16 was retired in 1983, ending the fixed-wing water landing era.[10] Many of the helicopters that were flown by the Coast Guard also had amphibious capability. The Sikorsky HH-52 Seaguard and the HH-3 Pelican were two such helicopters. In 1983, the Coast Guard Rescue Swimmer Program was developed. This new capability obviated the need for water landings, and the Pelican and Seaguard were subsequently replaced by the non-amphibious HH-60 Jayhawk and the HH-65 Dolphin.[11]

Technology has greatly changed the world of search and rescue capabilities. From pigeons to forward-looking infrared cameras, the Coast Guard has moved to leverage technology to further enhance its airborne search and rescue capability. Since the birth of Coast Guard Aviation, sixty-one different fixed-wing aircraft have been, at some point, part of the Coast Guard's inventory. Another seventeen different helicopters have been in service over time. This story is about one of these helicopters, the HH-60 Jayhawk.

3

THE HELICOPTER

If you are in trouble anywhere in the world, an airplane can fly over and drop flowers, but a helicopter can land and save your life.
—*Igor Sikorsky*

I gor Sikorsky was born in Kiev and immigrated to the United States following the Bolshevik Revolution. He then formed the Sikorsky Aircraft Company and developed what was described as the nation's first functional helicopter, taking to the air in 1939.

In 1941, the Coast Guard took a serious interest in developing a helicopter for search and rescue operations. But it would be World War II that brought the Coast Guard into rotary wing aviation. CDR William J. Kossler, who was the chief of the Aviation Engineering Division at Coast Guard Headquarters in Washington, D.C., witnessed Igor Sikorsky's test flight of his XR-4 prototype on April 20, 1942. Impressed with the craft, he invited CDR W.A. Burton, the commanding officer of Coast Guard Air Station Brooklyn, to witness a test flight.

CDR Burton wrote in his report what he witnessed:

The helicopter, in its present stage of development, has many of the advantages of the blimp and few of the disadvantages. It hovers and maneuvers with more facility in rough air than the blimp. It can land and take-off in less space. It does not require a large ground-handling crew. It does not need a large hanger. There is sufficient range—about two hours—in this particular model to make its use entirely practical for harbor patrol and other Coast Guard duties.

This report marked the beginning of the Coast Guard's significant involvement in the development of rotary-winged aircraft.

Burton's Executive Officer, CDR Frank Erickson, was the next officer to witness a Sikorsky demonstration, although, this time, Sikorsky flew the VS-300. Erickson immediately saw the capabilities of the rotary-winged aircraft in search and rescue operations. Faced with general indifference from other pilots, Coast Guard Headquarters and the U.S. Navy, Erickson decided to promote the antisubmarine and convoy protection possibilities of the new craft in his report to headquarters. The "higher-ups" began to show some interest.

After the Commandant of the Coast Guard VADM Russell R. Waesche saw a flight demonstration, he conferred with ADM Ernest J. King, USN, and King issued a directive that placed "the responsibility for the seagoing development of the helicopter [with] the U.S. Coast Guard."[12] This began the Coast Guard's role in developing the helicopter for use in a variety of applications for all military services.

It was Erickson who piloted the first lifesaving mission by helicopter.

Over the ensuing years, the Coast Guard has had seventeen rotary wing aircraft in its inventory. Ten of these bore the name Sikorsky. Over time, these aircraft became more reliable, more powerful, had longer "legs" (operational range) and greater lift capability. In the early 1960s, the Sikorsky HH-52 Seaguard was the workhorse for coastal search and rescue as well as

First Coast Guard Helicopter Detachment, Sikorsky Helicopter Airport, Bridgeport, Connecticut, July 7, 1943. *Left to right*: Seaman E.H. Frauenberger, Petty Officer First Class J.A. Boone, Chief Petty Officer L. Brzycki, Lieutenant A.N. Fisher, Lieutenant Commander F.A. Erickson, Lieutenant O.M. Helgren, Chief Petty Officer O.F. Berry and Petty Officer First Class W.J. Woodcock. *U.S. Coast Guard photograph.*

Coast Guard photograph, Petty Officer Third Class Joshua Canup.

operating with cutters and icebreakers in various other missions. The H-3 Pelican was introduced in 1968, providing more lift capacity and greater range and speed. As mentioned previously, both the Seaguard and Pelican had water landing capability.

In 1990, the Sikorsky HH-60 Jayhawk was introduced to replace the H-3. This was the end of the Coast Guard's amphibious helicopter era. Today, however, the MH-60 aircraft has become the long legs lifter for the Coast Guard fleet. In addition to state-of-the-art avionics, the Coast Guard's version employs a 600-pound rescue hoist able to deploy rescue swimmers and hoist rescue litters and baskets. Since the very first hoist, thousands of people in distress have been on the end of the line as they have been hoisted to safety. Standard crewing for the HH-60 Jayhawk involves a pilot, a copilot, a flight mechanic and a rescue swimmer. The aircraft has six additional seats for potential "rescuees." With over three thousand shaft horsepower from two engines, it can carry over 6,500 pounds of fuel. Extra fuel external drop tanks can be easily fitted for extended range, longer hover times, poor flying conditions or, in the case of the *SeaBreeze* rescue, all of the above.

4

KILL DEVIL HILLS

I n 1900, the Wright brothers began researching locations from where they could begin their flying experiments. Kitty Hawk, North Carolina, a tiny coastal fishing village of approximately three hundred people at the turn of the century, would come to suit their needs.

The Wrights desired a number of conditions in order to successfully experiment with controlled flight. First, they needed steady winds. Second, they needed an area with high sand dunes from which to glide. Third, they needed limited obstructions (trees, buildings, et cetera) and, lastly, they needed isolation to experiment unencumbered.

Kitty Hawk's average wind speed is fifteen to twenty miles per hour, ideal for the Wrights' experiments. In 1900, the area was primarily sand flats and sand dunes, with only a smattering of man-made structures (the U.S. Life-Saving Station, a weather station and post office and a small amount of private homes), making the area ideal for the isolation they desired. In addition, Kill Devil Hills, located four miles south of town, provided massive dunes from which to glide and an abundance of sand to act as a cushion for crash landings.

Wilbur arrived in Kitty Hawk in a small fishing schooner on September 13, 1900; Orville arrived eleven days later. Just three days prior to arriving, Wilbur wrote to his father, Milton, to explain his reasons for choosing the area.

I chose Kitty Hawk because it seemed the place which most clearly met the required conditions....At Kitty Hawk, which is on the narrow bar separating the sound from the ocean, there are neither hills nor trees so that it offers a safe place for practice. Also, the wind there is stronger than any place near home and is almost constant.

Initially residing with postmaster William Tate and his family (who would become instrumental in assisting the Wrights), the brothers set up their own camp a half mile south of town on October 4 and began their experiments in earnest.[13] In the following years, the Wrights conducted hundreds of preflight gliding experiments to reach their ultimate objective, powered flight.

Members of the U.S Life-Saving Service Station No. 13, Station Kill Devil Hills, North Carolina, assisted Orville and Wilbur Wright by hauling lumber and carrying mail. They also assisted in the building of the monorail "runway." As the project neared completion, they were present to witness and assist in this historic event.

On December 17, 1903, the men placed their flying machine on the monorail, and then, the brothers set the engine's ignition and turned the propellers. Orville's first flight lasted all of twelve seconds and covered a distance of 120 feet; it wasn't much of a flight, but it was enough to put the brothers in the history books. The surfmen then helped drag the Wright flyer back to the start of the monorail three more times, with each flight lasting longer and covering more distance. The fourth flight was the longest, with the machine flying for over 852 feet in fifty-nine seconds. It was slightly damaged after landing, however, and while the brothers discussed repairing it, a strong gust of wind blew across the beach and threatened to flip the flyer over. Surfman Daniels risked his life by jumping on a wing to attempt to hold the flyer down, but the wind gust was too much, and it lifted the machine

U.S Life-Saving Service Station No. 13, Station Kill Devil Hills, North Carolina. *Photograph courtesy of Library of Congress, Orville Wright collection.*

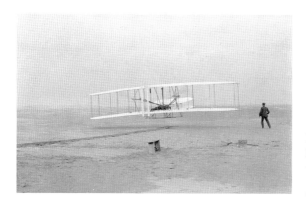

First flight glass-plate photograph. *Courtesy of Library of Congress, Orville Wright collection. Photograph taken by Surfman Daniels.*

and Daniels end over end. Daniels finally slipped free from the tumbling flyer and fell 15 feet to the ground, injuring his ribs and getting a few bruises, but he was otherwise unharmed.[14] (Surfman Daniels of the Kill Devil Hills Station was the person who took the famous photograph that showed the world the first powered flight.)

At the time, Kitty Hawk, North Carolina, was the closest town to the site of the Wright brothers' enterprise. However, in 1932, a monument was built at Kill Devil Hills as a memorial to the Wright brothers. It is currently administered by the National Park Service.

Kill Devil Hills is an integral part of our story not only from the contributions of the surfmen to this historic event but also the Coast Guard's continued involvement in the annual recognition of the anniversary of powered flight.

Congress, by a joint resolution that was approved on December 17, 1963, designated December 17 of each year Wright Brothers Day and authorized and requested the President to annually issue a proclamation, inviting the people of the United States to observe that day with appropriate ceremonies and activities.[15] Among these appropriate activities is a flyover of various aircraft representing the historic airplane community as well as the armed services of the United States. Every year, the Coast Guard participates in the flyover with aircraft from Coast Guard Air Station Elizabeth City, weather permitting.

In the year 2000, there was a problem.

RESCUE RABBIT

Northeast North Carolina has played a major role in aviation since the Wright brothers used Elizabeth City as a jumping off point for their journey from Dayton to Kitty Hawk in 1903. The Coast Guard base at Elizabeth City continues that tradition.

Beginning in 1939 and continuing to the present day, Elizabeth City is the site of the only airport owned and operated by the United States Coast Guard. In response to the buildup prior to World War II, the base spent its first five years under the operational and administrative control of the U.S. Navy. During the war, the base population reached 8,500 personnel, and it became a major maintenance depot for flying boats. The Air Station was responsible for antisubmarine patrols as well as search and rescue missions for the major shipping lanes from just off of the Outer Banks of North Carolina to Norfolk, Virginia.

After the war, the base was turned over to the U.S. Coast Guard, which made immediate use of the extensive maintenance facilities by creating the Aircraft Repair and Supply Base in 1947.

Air Station Elizabeth City was at the forefront of the helicopter's introduction into the SAR mission and home to the Rotary Wing Development Squadron, which was then led by legendary Commander Frank "Swede" Erickson. This introduction was not without controversy and resistance. One of the Air Station's commanding officers was Captain Donald MacDiarmid, a champion of the flying boat who fought Erickson to determine the future of aircraft in SAR missions. For most of the 1950s and the early 1960s, the flying boats were the gold standard for the Coast Guard's air-sea rescue inventory. But over time, the technical improvements in rotary flight would win out. Needless to say, the flying boat, today, is merely a historical infatuation; the helicopter, however, is here to stay.

By the mid-1960s, the Aircraft Repair and Supply Base had built a solid reputation as a premier rework facility. Most U.S. Coast Guard aircraft came through its two huge hangars on the east end of the 880-acre complex. Sikorsky HH-52 Sea Guard and HH-3 Pelican helicopters were all disassembled, reworked and rebuilt onsite. The same can be said for Grumman HU-16 (the Coast Guard's last flying boat), the Fairchild C-123 and, recently, the Lockheed C-130 Hercules. Initially, the base also served as a boot camp for all of the Coast Guard's aviation rates.

In 2000, Coast Guard Air Station Elizabeth City was one of the service's largest Air Stations. With a fleet of three Sikorsky HH-60J Jayhawk helicopters and five C-130 Hercules aircraft, the unit's missions included support of law enforcement, marine environmental protection, hurricane relief, treaties enforcement and search and rescue.[16]

As is true with most military units, Coast Guard Air Station Elizabeth City needed a unique patch, descriptive of its main mission. In 1941, the patch was designed by a Warner Brothers cartoonist. It reflects part of the World War II messaging effort of the era by both Walt Disney and Warner Brothers. They designed patches for both the Coast Guard and the U.S. Navy, using their cartoon characters to show support of the war effort. The Air Station Elizabeth City patch depicts Bugs Bunny as Rescue Rabbit, ready to perform the Air Station's primary mission of search and rescue. The original patch has a solid yellow background, the same color that was used on Coast Guard aircraft, which had a solid yellow stripe bordered by black on an otherwise unpainted aluminum fuselage. But for Coast Guard aircraft, this color scheme would not remain.

In May 1963, President Kennedy recommended that the Coast Guard should be the first to get an imagery overhaul. It was called the Integrated Visual Identification Program. The design firm of Raymond Loewy/William Snaith Inc. was contracted to develop an identification device. The result was the color bar concept known as the diagonal racing stripe logo. This new design was tested on cutters and facilities at the Coast Guard's Seventh District in Florida. Cutters, buoy tenders, vehicles and buildings at Base Miami all tested the new racing stripe logo. Helicopters and fix-winged aircraft were also included in the test at Air Station Elizabeth City. With the successful test and a few modifications to the logo and font, on April

Above: U.S. Coast Guard photograph.

Left: Image courtesy of Craig Neubecker.

6, 1967, Commandant of the Coast Guard Admiral Edwin Roland issued Instruction 5030.5, which ordered service-wide implementation of the Visual Identification System. The racing stripe logo became official and was added to all Coast Guard vehicles, buildings, stationary, signage, stations, cutters, boats and aircraft.

Eventually, all assets in the Coast Guard adopted the new symbol. By 1975, the Coast Guard's training ship *Eagle* remained the last service asset without the racing stripe logo. The nation was preparing for a bicentennial celebration, and the *Eagle* was to serve as the host ship of OpSail76. The Coast Guard leadership saw an opportunity to present the racing stripe logo, which would distinguish the *Eagle* from all the other tall ships.[17]

So, it was time to change the Air Station patch. In 2000, LTJG Neubecker, who we will meet again later, redesigned the patch with Rescue Rabbit superimposed on the "new" racing stripe and in front of the Coast Guard's wings of gold. The two aircraft types, the HH-60J Jayhawk and the HC-130H Hercules, were added along with the Coast Guard's motto *Semper Paratus* (always ready).

Only two Coast Guard Air Stations continue to use the original World War II art for mascots, Air Station Elizabeth City and Air Station Sacramento, which proudly displays Yosemite Sam.

Coast Guard Cutter *Eagle. U.S. Coast Guard photograph.*

Top: Image courtesy of Craig Neubecker. Bottom: Image courtesy of Michael McCleary.

© Touchstone Pictures.

In 1984, Congress directed the Coast Guard to establish a rescue swimmer program. The decision came as a result of the 1983 sinking of the M/V *Marine Electric*, which involved the loss of thirty-one crew members. The incident was a catalyst to bring about significant changes to enhance maritime safety, including the establishment of the rescue swimmer program. The program is located at the Aviation Technical Training Center (ATTC), which is adjacent to Coast Guard Air Station Elizabeth City. Every year, more than one hundred enlisted men and women sign up for the extensive, physically demanding eighteen-week program, and fewer than half actually complete the program. AST1 Darren Reeves and AST3 Robert Florisi are program graduates and are part of this story.

In 2006, Air Station Elizabeth City was the backdrop for the film *The Guardian*. The main character is played by Kevin Costner, but many of the supporting actors, including ATTC instructors, helicopter pilots and support personnel, are actual U.S. Coast Guard rescue swimmers, pilots and ground personnel. One of those pilots was LT Dan Molthen, who we will meet again later.

IN JUNE 1998, COAST Guard Air Station Elizabeth City got a new commanding officer, Captain John R. Odom III. (His "go by" is Bob.) Of average height for his generation, he affects a commanding presence without decree and is well respected by those who serve with him. An understudy of leaders throughout his career, he knows that leadership is the ability to bring forth the best of a person's talents, and he does it well.

Bob is a graduate of the Virginia Military Institute (VMI).[18] After graduation, he went to the Marine Corps Officer Candidate School in Quantico, Virginia, where he received his commission as a Second Lieutenant in the fall of 1966. At that time, the Marine Corps desperately needed helicopter pilots, so most of the aviation candidates skipped the Basic School and headed directly to flight school at Pensacola. He was "winged" at Pensacola on January 23, 1968, as a Naval Aviator and soon departed for Vietnam, where he was assigned to the Marine Corps squadron flying twin-rotor CH-46s out of Quang Tri. He later received four Air Medals and the Distinguished Flying Cross for his duty in Vietnam. Eventually, he transitioned to flying C-130s, and after nearly seven and a half years in the Marine Corps, he was released from active duty.

A year and a half later, Bob entered the Coast Guard and was assigned to Coast Guard Air Station Elizabeth City as a C-130 pilot.

> ODOM. *Both of my parents, an uncle and an aunt were in the Coast Guard during World War II. However, I am the first aviator and career officer. I had run gauntlets at VMI, Quantico, Pensacola and Vietnam in a way that really stood me in good stead in the Coast Guard throughout my career. I understood effective leadership because I had been taught and mentored by some of the best.*

Tested early in his tour of duty, Captain Odom and his command would have to respond to the devastation of Hurricane Floyd. The hurricane produced torrential rainfall along the North Carolina coast and inland in areas that had already been saturated by extensive rainfall from Hurricane Dennis a few weeks earlier. Most rivers in the area surpassed five-hundred-year flood levels.

Hurricane Floyd claimed fifty-seven lives and caused over $6 billion in damage. Helicopters from Coast Guard Air Station Elizabeth City worked with double crews for five days to rescue people who were stranded in high water.

> ODOM. *We had a culture at the Air Station that is hard to describe. Perhaps it was a deep-seated pride, born of professional excellence and a hard work ethic. No one spoke directly about it, but everyone from the pilots to the hangar deck crews felt it. It was one of the best units I served in and as commanding officer in my final tour. I could not have asked for a better command.*

In 2000, Captain Odom and his command were tested again.

6

Y2K

Our story takes place in 2000.

The turn of the century or the "dawn of the new millennium" brought unexpected challenges to the emerging age of computers and computer-controlled infrastructure. Early in 1999, Defense Department officials were warning that the Y2K problem, also known as the "millennium bug," could be the "electronic equivalent of the El Niño," and the full impact of the problem may be experienced globally. Awareness of it reached the highest levels of Congress and the federal government in the context of national security. The Coast Guard, as an agency within the Department of Transportation (DOT), responded to requirements funded by Congress and directed by the administration to form a working group that was to be part of the federal community of policy working committees that was headed from the White House and funded by Congress.

Federal agencies, as well as business and industry agencies, scrambled to identify and adapt to a pending but amorphous Armageddon. Tests of the existing systems in the United States portrayed frightening results, such as two million gallons of sewage being released in a park in California and numerous examples of security systems locking buildings and not allowing anyone to enter. The Coast Guard tested what it could of the over forty computer systems that did things like plot SAR missions, model oil spill trajectory projections and other computerized programs that supported critical Coast Guard missions. Some programs, however, simply could not be tested because they were so old that coding changes would not allow access. With the worst-case scenario of losing connectivity internally and with other agencies added to the possible loss of stored data, the scare was enough to establish contingency teams with experts to both initiate steps to reduce or eliminate any impact and then address problems that surfaced once the calendar year started anew.

The author of this book first met LCDR Chuck Adams in 1985. He was one of the author's officers at Coast Guard Reserve Unit San Luis Obispo, California. Their unit mission was to augment two aging Coast Guard Cutters (CGC) in Morro Bay, CGC *Cape Wash* and CGC *Cape Hedge*. Both cutters were over thirty years old and at the end of their service lives, but they made excellent training platforms for the unit. Chuck was an anomaly in terms of Coast Guard officers.

The vast majority of those who serve as commissioned officers are either sourced through the Coast Guard Academy or the Coast Guard's Officer Candidate School. Many of the Coast Guard's pilots come in as transfers from other services. Only a trickle come to the Coast Guard through the Maritime Academy Graduate (MARGRAD) program. Graduates of the U.S. Merchant Marine Academy at Kings Point and the six state-sponsored maritime academies (Massachusetts, Maine, New York, Great Lakes, Texas A&M and California) are sought by the Coast Guard due to their focused training in maritime industry affairs, marine transportation, vessel management and engineering and because they are licensed U.S. Merchant Marine officers. They enter the Coast Guard as reserve officers and are placed on three years of active duty.

Chuck was a Kings Point graduate, but before coming to the Coast Guard, he entered the training program for the only United States–flagged nuclear power merchant ship, the NS *Savannah*, part of the first Atomic Ship Transport Program. Eventually, the low price of oil would end the program simply because the *Savannah* could not compete when the conventional fuel was so cheap. After a few assignments in Guam and Kwajalein Island working for the Navy's Third Fleet, he came back into the nuclear business at Hanford, Washington, working on the startup for the Fast Flux Test Facility. Later, he was certified as a senior reactor operator instructor (SROI) in the Westinghouse training program, and he took a position at Diablo Canyon, the Pacific Gas & Electric nuclear plant on the central California coast. This background and experience in the field gave him the insight he needed to evaluate the worldwide reports in the power field and the computerized systems that control them. Still a Coast Guard reserve officer, he was about to play a critical role in addressing the millennium bug.

The Coast Guard Commandant at the time was Admiral James Loy. Jim was well respected for his leadership and represented the Coast Guard well among its sister services. His motto, "preparation equals performance," became his brand. His demeanor displayed a professional confidence and command presence, but he was also personable and valued input from even the lowest-ranking enlisted "coasties." Before making flag rank, he had commanded several Coast Guard Cutters, including the *Point Lomas* on combat patrols in Vietnam; Coast Guard Cutter *Valiant*, homeported in Galveston, Texas; and Coast Guard Cutter *Midgett*, homeported in San Francisco, California.

Among Loy's top priorities were leadership training and the modernization of the Coast Guard's aging fleet. He would appoint Rear Admiral Pat Stillman to head up the new Integrated Deepwater System Program, a twenty-five-year program to replace all or most of the United States Coast Guard's legacy systems with state-of-the-art equipment, including aircraft, ships and logistics and command and control systems. But in 1999, he also had another priority to address: Y2K. And for that, he needed a team of specialists.

The Commandant's office was located at Coast Guard Headquarters at Buzzard Point, just next to Fort McNair and the National War College in Washington, D.C. Historically, this area was used as a city dump, and later, it would be the site of the first federal execution of a woman, Mary Surratt (and three other coconspirators to the Lincoln assassination), on hastily built gallows at Fort McNair. The Commandant's office overlooked the Anacostia River to the south. It provided good views of the Sikorsky Sea King helicopters with the call sign of Marine One taking off and landing at Anacostia Naval Air Station, shuttling the President and other dignitaries to and from Andrews Air Force Base, the home of Air Force One.

The Coast Guard Headquarters building had seven floors, but the elevators in the building were preprogrammed to not stop at the fourth floor, even if a person mistakenly pressed the button for that floor. That is because there were no offices on the fourth floor; it was a dark, unheated storage area. It would soon become the home to an elite team of reservists who were to address the Y2K issue. Wanting to find the best people to address the issue, head up a team and develop prevention and response plans, the Coast Guard turned to its reserve component, where it looked for the right people with the civilian skills to meet the challenge. Chuck Adams was called to active duty, and he and his team were then the only occupants of the fourth floor.

Because Y2K posed a threat to the Secret Internet Protocol Router Network (SIPRNet), Chuck needed a top secret security clearance to do the work. Early on, he was designated as the DOT's representative on the interagency policy committee and initiated, in both the DOT and the Coast Guard, the planning to monitor critical fields to determine if Y2K was active in these two agencies. This model was later adopted by the White House organization and was put out to the entire federal government.

Only two of the Coast Guard's computer systems were actually affected by the millennium bug, and new systems were brought in to replace them. Chuck's team was disbanded in January 2000, but he was asked to stay on to develop the Coast Guard's Continuity of Operation Plan (COOP). Later, he moved on to the new Department of Homeland Security to develop its COOP plan, and then, he moved on to the U.S. Senate to do the same thing.

The Y2K issue quickly faded into history as the year 2000 brought other headline-grabbing news and tragedies to the United States and other parts of the world.

Air France Flight 4590, a Concorde aircraft, crashed into a hotel just after taking off from Paris, killing all 109 aboard and 4 in the hotel. The Russian submarine *Kursk* sank in the Barents Sea during a Russian naval exercise, resulting in the deaths of all 118 men on board. The Greek ferry *Express Samina* sank off the island of Paros, killing 80 passengers. In the port city of Aden, Yemen, the USS *Cole* was badly damaged when two Al-Qaeda suicide bombers drove a small boat loaded with explosives next to the *Cole*. The explosion killed 17 crew members and wounded another 39. Later that year, Singapore Airlines Flight 006 collided with construction equipment in the Chiang Kai Shek International Airport, resulting in 83 deaths.

But closer to home, the Coast Guard responded to another tragedy in early 2000. On January 31, Alaska Airlines Flight 261 was flying from Puerto Vallarta, Mexico, to Seattle–Tacoma International Airport with an intermediate stop at San Francisco International Airport. It was carrying eighty-three passengers and a crew of five. On that date, it crashed into the Pacific Ocean several miles off the California coast, near Anacapa Island. The Coast Guard launched a massive response and designated Captain George Wright, Commanding Officer of Marine Safety Office, Los Angeles–Long Beach, to be the Coast Guard face before the media. This would later change to Vice Admiral Tom Collins, the Pacific Area Commander who, after several days of seemingly endless searching, halted the search efforts. Everyone aboard Flight 261 was lost.

The Coast Guard would get another call to respond to a certain disaster in 2000—this time, with a different outcome.

7
FOOTPRINTS OF THOSE BEFORE US

The turn of the century also presented the Coast Guard with the opportunity to look back on its many heroic rescues of the previous one hundred years. After an extensive review of thousands of rescues, the Coast Guard released a "U.S. Coast Guard Media Advisory" with the following headline "U.S. COAST GUARD DECLARES ITS TOP RESCUES OF THE CENTURY."[19]

The advisory listed the "top ten" rescues numerically. One of these rescues involves a main character in our story. We will meet him again.

NUMBER TEN

On November 17, 1994, a family of four traveling in a sixty-four-foot-long sailboat, the *Marine Flower II*, left Little Creek, Virginia, en route to Bermuda. They encountered fifty-mile-per-hour winds and twenty-foot-high seas four hundred miles off the Virginia Coast during Hurricane Gordon. Aboard the boat were a husband and his wife, their thirteen-year-old daughter and their four-month-old son. A Coast Guard helicopter from Air Station Elizabeth City, North Carolina, was sent on the rescue mission.

The aircraft commander was LCDR Dave Gundersen; LT Dan Molthen, who we will meet again, was the copilot; Bobby Blackwell was the flight mechanic; and ASMT3 Mario Vittone was the rescue swimmer. The distance offshore was well beyond the fuel capacity of the helicopter, so the crew made a fuel stop on the transiting aircraft carrier USS *America*. Dan Molthen, a U.S. Naval Academy graduate, earned his wings in the Navy, and after nine years, he transitioned to the Coast Guard. He never imagined that he would be back on the deck of a Navy vessel while on a Coast Guard rescue mission.

Once they were on scene, the helicopter crew surveyed the sailboat and determined that the vessel's masts and rigging were in danger of tangling the rescue basket and hoisting cable, so they decided to put rescue swimmer Vittone into the water next to the vessel, allowing him to board the vessel and assist in hoisting. With the sailboat's mainsail still deployed, the vessel quickly pulled away from the rescue swimmer, who was unable to reach it by swimming. A decision was made to retrieve the rescue swimmer and discuss an alternative approach. The rescue swimmer deployed again, but this time, the four passengers, including the four-month-old baby, had to enter the water, and the rescue swimmer assisted them into the rescue basket. The mother and baby were the first to enter the water. The mother secured the infant to her chest prior to jumping into the water. Rescue swimmer Vittone reached them, and in spite of heavy seas and high winds, they were put into the basket and retrieved. The daughter and father were then retrieved separately.

Once aboard the helicopter, the family was stabilized, but critically low fuel was again an issue. Gundersen and Molthen headed back to *America* for more fuel before returning to shore. All of the Coast Guard aircrew received the Coast Guard's Distinguished Flying Cross medal for their actions. This was the first Distinguished Flying Cross medal for Dan Molthen:

Citation to Accompany the Award of
the Distinguished Flying Cross
to
Lieutenant (Junior Grade) Daniel J. Molthen
United States Coast Guard

Lieutenant (Junior Grade) MOLTHEN is cited for extraordinary achievement while participating in aerial flight on 17 November 1994 while serving as copilot aboard Coast Guard HH-60J helicopter CGNR 6034. The aircrew was engaged in the rescue of a family of four from the sailing vessel **MARINE FLOWER II** *that was being thrashed by Hurricane Gordon, 400 miles off the coast of North Carolina. Lieutenant (Junior Grade) MOLTHEN's meticulous preflight planning,* *constant reevaluations of the strong, shifting winds, verifications of fuel burn rates, and continual updates of groundspeed, were critical to the successful completion of both an extremely difficult rescue, and long range, 800-plus-mile, over-water flight in hurricane conditions. His extraordinary aeronautical ability was evident during the day and night landings aboard the USS AMERICA. With seas breaking over the bow, he expertly guided the helicopter down to safe landings in conditions that were well out of limits for carrier flight operations. His diligent monitoring of aircraft systems, altitudes, and obstacles allowed the pilot to better concentrate on hoisting the mother and 4-month-old infant out of the storm-tossed seas. His efforts allowed the crew to complete the rescue evolution expeditiously when fuel endurance was critical. With the rescue completed, he navigated the helicopter back to the USS AMERICA. Lieutenant (Junior Grade) MOLTHEN's actions, aeronautical skill, and valor were instrumental in the rescue of four persons. His courage, judgment, and devotion to duty are most heartily commended and are in keeping with the highest traditions of the United States Coast Guard.*

NUMBER NINE

The Coast Guard rescued seven from tugs and tows off the coast of Fort Lauderdale, Florida, in 1997. The tug *Samson*, pulling two barges and another tugboat, began sinking thirty-five miles northeast of Fort Lauderdale on April 23, 1997. An HH-65A helicopter from Coast Guard Air Station Miami was the first on scene and hoisted the four-man crew off the *Samson*. The helicopter then hoisted the watch stander off the second tugboat after he broke tow with the barges because it was foundering in six-foot seas with twenty-knot winds. A forty-one-foot-long Coast Guard boat from Station Fort Lauderdale rescued the two men who were on the barges.

NUMBER EIGHT

The Coast Guard rescued a crew of four from a sinking fishing vessel, *Gambler*, off the coast of Massachusetts on April 3, 1994. The sixty-five-foot-long fishing boat *Gambler* called the Coast Guard at 1400 on Easter Sunday, reporting it had four to five feet of water in its engine room. A Coast Guard helicopter lowered a dewatering pump, but it was unable to keep up with the incoming water. A forty-one-foot-long boat from Coast Guard Station Scituate evacuated all four fishermen from the trawler just minutes before the boat sank.

Number Seven

A Coast Guard Auxiliarist jumped into the water to help rescue people in Fort Lauderdale, Florida, on April 6, 1997. Frank Mauro, a member of the Coast Guard's volunteer arm, the Coast Guard Auxiliary, received the Gold Lifesaving Medal for his heroic efforts in helping rescue nine victims who were forced into the water after the current drove their boat under a moored barge in the Intracoastal Waterway. Mauro, who was serving as a crewman aboard a forty-one-foot-long Coast Guard boat dove into the water when he saw a struggling young girl who was about to be forced under the bow of the barge. As he was about to save her, three panicking adult victims grabbed him to avoid being sucked under the barge themselves.

Mauro was able to pull all four from the powerful current in front of the barge, and he got all of them safely onto a Coast Guard boat. An active-duty Coast Guard member also dove in to assist with the rescue. In all, seven of the nine were pulled to safety; two victims died.

Number Six

Two boaters were rescued in heavy surf off the coast of Newport, Oregon, on June 8, 1996. A fourteen-foot-long aluminum boat with two aboard capsized near the Yaquina River Jetties. A helicopter from Coast Guard Air Facility Newport and two boats from Coast Guard Station Yaquina Bay area were on the scene within minutes. The helicopter lowered its rescue swimmer, who achieved a physical hold of one of the men but lost his grip after waves from the eight- to ten-foot-high breaking surf crash over the stern. After the rescue swimmer resurfaced and relocated the man, he attached the man to a helicopter hoist cable, and both were hoisted to an awaiting emergency team that was positioned on the jetties. During the helicopter hoist, the waves began pushing the overturned boat and the second man away from the jetties. The forty-one-foot-long motor lifeboat maneuvered to the second man and pulled him aboard.

Number Five

Coast Guard Signalman First Class Douglas Munro rescued Marines at Guadalcanal.

Munro, alongside other Coast Guardsmen, was responsible for navigating the landing of a craft full of U.S. Marine forces along the coast. The landing craft not only allowed for troop movements during the war effort, but it also transferred crucial supplies to and from the troops during the height of battle.

A month after the initial landing at Guadalcanal, Munro joined twenty-four other U.S. Coast Guard and U.S. Navy personnel who were assigned to Lunga Point Base, which served as a staging area for all the landing craft throughout the area. A month into the campaign, U.S. Marine Lieutenant Colonel Lewis B. "Chesty" Puller embarked three companies of U.S. Marines into landing craft in an effort to push past their defensive line and take control of the western region of Guadalcanal.

Munro, just two weeks short of his twenty-third birthday, took control of ten landing craft to move Puller's men from the staging area to the western coast. After successfully landing and moving five hundred yards inland, Munro took all but one of the landing craft and returned to the staging area. Just an hour after landing on the western coast of the island, the U.S. Marine forces were overcome by Japanese bombing raids, driving out their gunfire support and causing the situation to quickly deteriorate.

Just two hours later, the plight of the Marine forces became known. The troops were being driven back to the beach, but many did not have access to radios to inform supporting units and request assistance. A single "HELP" spelled out in T-shirts on the ridge near the beach provided a sign of what the Marines needed.

Munro, back at the staging area but knowing of the Marines' needs, volunteered to navigate the same landing craft to rescue the Marines from enemy fire. Nearing the beach, the landing craft themselves came under enemy fire, causing many casualties and making the mission more dangerous by the minute. Despite all this, Munro directed the landing craft to push forward, even with Japanese forces gaining ground and nearing the beach.

As the Marines re-embarked on the landing craft, Munro recognized the dangerous situation that was developing, as Japanese forces were firing from only five hundred yards beyond the beach where Marine forces were retreating. Munro immediately navigated his vessel between the enemy fire and the Marine forces, providing much-needed cover for the Marines. With his efforts, all of the Marines, including the wounded, were safely taken off the island. With this, the landing craft began to return to the staging area, but Munro noticed one of the craft, full of Marines, was grounded on the beach and not far from enemy forces. Munro returned and directed a landing tank to pull the craft off the beach, and just twenty minutes later, the craft was free and able to head out to sea. At this same time, the Japanese forces began firing machine gun rounds at the final craft as they retreated. Though warnings were shouted, Munro was struck with a single bullet. He died before the forces returned to the staging area.

In a letter dated just five days later, the commanding officer of the unit wrote to inform Munro's parents of their son's heroism and death. The letter said, "Upon regaining consciousness, his only question was 'Did they get off?' So, he died with a smile on his face and the full knowledge that he had successfully accomplished a dangerous mission."

For his efforts, Munro was posthumously awarded the Medal of Honor, and he is the only member of the Coast Guard to have been given the honor. Today, seventy-three years later, Munro's legacy lives on. He is remembered and honored by every member of the Coast Guard for his selfless devotion to duty and heroism.[20]

NUMBER 4

In 1956, there was a Coast Guard rescue that caught the attention of the entire nation. The following is an excerpt from the Pan American Historical Foundation publication *Clipper*:

On October 16, Captain Richard Ogg was piloting his Pan American Stratocruiser high across the Pacific Ocean on a routine flight from Honolulu to San Francisco. Thousands of feet below, Commander William K. Earle was patrolling a lonely spot in the ocean (Ocean Station November) with the U.S. Coast Guard Cutter *Pontchartrain*. Within minutes of these two vessels passing in the night, the captain and the commander would become responsible for planning the rescue and safety of thirty-one souls onboard clipper *Sovereign of the Skies*. Here's how it happened.

It was just a little after 0300, when the nighttime silence was shattered by an urgent communication on the ship's radio receiver.

> *This is Clipper 943! We are having emergency engine trouble! May have to ditch! Please alert your crew and stand by to assist us!*

The stunned night watch leaped into action but not before responding.

> *Roger your message, Clipper 943. Will give you continuous beacon. Our crew is being alerted.*

Even though the ship and its crew were fully prepared and intensively trained for a "ditching," the dreaded D-word rang an ominous tone. The phrase "all hands on deck" was coined for just such an occasion, and in no time, the ship was awake with activity, with each man to his station.

Another communiqué came through:

> *This is Clipper 943! I'm losing altitude fast! I'm coming in on your beacon and will try to make it to the ship. Can you give me a recommended ditch heading?*

According to Commander Earle, the most important factor involved in ditching is the ditch heading. The ditching course must be selected with great care after detailed study of the wind and swell conditions. The optimum strategy is for the plane to land upwind and across a swell.

The calculations were quickly computed, and the heading was set for "245 degrees true." A previously prepared ditch check-off list was followed by a flurry of organized activity—with only minutes to go before the ditching. The ship indicated the suggested landing path by dropping water lights overboard and releasing star shells.[21]

Meanwhile, Captain Ogg was doing his own calculations as he orbited over the cutter, which was then bearing its beacons upward. He determined that because he still had a large amount of fuel on the plane and that its altitude could be held without too much difficulty, he would try to postpone the ditching until daylight. Landing a plane on the ocean under any condition is terrifying, but at night, with only artificial illumination, it would be doubly so. Then there would be more time for both the Pan American and the

Pontchartrain crews to review and be ready for every possible contingency. The captain and the commander kept up continuous radio conversation, going over the procedures again and again.

The passengers aboard the clipper had been kept fully informed of developments. They were told to don their life jackets and remove their shoes before being moved up to the forward section of the airplane. It was a tribute to the seven Pan American crew members that there was no sign of panic in the passengers, who numbered twenty-four, including three small children.

Because of the crew schedule, new calculations had to be made for the ditch heading. So, at first light, Commander Earle radioed Captain Ogg:

> *Good morning, Captain. It's a beautiful day down here. The easterly swells have increased a bit, and I suggest we now shift to 330 degrees as a heading. We are prepared to mark out a landing path on this new heading with fire extinguisher foam whenever you want it.*

Captain Ogg responded:

> *They're already up here. My gals have done a great job, and the passengers are quite calm. I think I'll wait until my gasoline is almost gone to reduce the chance of fire. This will probably be in about an hour, but I'll give you plenty of advance warning.*

Commander Earle advised the captain that they would be having breakfast together before long and then asked how he liked his eggs.

Finally, full daylight arrived. With his gasoline nearly gone, Captain Ogg circled to begin his last run. The *Pontchartrain* got underway and, at full speed, laid a two-mile-long foam path on the ditch heading as men began piling into boats, hauling rubber life rafts up to the rail and flopping Jacob's ladders over the side. Swimmers and deck rescue details were standing by. All preparations had been made. This was the real one.

Commander Earle's last radio words to Captain Ogg were

> *You just set her down nice and easy, as close to us as possible, and we'll have you out in no time. Good luck and God bless you!*

Captain Ogg replied:

> *We have full confidence in you.*

Pan American Flight 942 landing in the Pacific Ocean on October 16, 1956. The Boeing 377 Stratocruiser lost power to two of its four engines and had to risk an emergency water landing. *William Simpson, U.S. Coast Guard photograph.*

At 0815, after nearly five hours of preparation, the plane touched down on the makeshift runway of water. It hit, bounced, hit again. The bow went down, and the tail came up and then broke off. Miraculously, survivors began climbing out onto the wings and launched life rafts.

Charging up at full speed, the *Pontchartrain* launched its boats. The first boat began picking up passengers within seven minutes after the plane touched down. After checking the sinking fuselage for other survivors, the second boat took aboard the occupants of the life rafts. As the rescue boats were slowly picking their way through the crash debris, the commander and his crew were ready to receive the survivors.[22]

The first motorboat arrived with fourteen passengers—six men, six women and two children. The second boat was returning, and the magic number was seventeen, which should include another small child. "Please God," prayed Commander Earle. "Let there be seventeen aboard!"

It seemed an eternity before the boat tied up to unload its precious cargo. As the men and women climbed up the ladders, the ship's crew began yelling out the count "Fourteen, fifteen, sixteen," and, finally, "seventeen!" A great cheer went up from the men on deck. Within twenty minutes of the ditching, the plane crew and passengers were aboard the cutter, none with serious injury. Commander Earle went to the public address system and choked out the words "All saved! All saved!"

Meanwhile, the whole world was waiting for word of the rescue. Once the thumbs-up sign was given, congratulatory messages to both the captain and the commander poured in from such people as the secretary of the treasury, Pan American Executives from all divisions, friends, family and colleagues. A United flight that was passing overhead transmitted, "The captain and crew of United 73 wish to be one of the first to offer their sincere gratitude and congratulations on your rescue today." Then came a barrage of requests from newsmen and radio commentators for personal accounts and interviews.

Shortly after the survivors were settled in with warm clothing, food and minor medical attention, the commander and the captain met. "We are all rightly grateful to you and your men," said the captain. According to Commander Earle, "Though we had a great deal to say to each other, this was not the time. We talked briefly about the condition of the passengers, and I invited him to join me for dinner that night." While there would be plenty of time for talk during the three-day trip to San Francisco, there also were many details to square away. Reports had to be written, and a complete critique of the operation had to be developed.

As the *Pontchartrain* drew close to San Francisco, another cutter met the ship and dropped off Coast Guard and Pan American officials, who brought along appropriate clothing for the survivors. Because they had lost everything in the airplane, they had been wearing Coast Guard–issued clothing. Just inside the Golden Gate Bridge, the *Pontchartrain* was met by fire boats spouting their water hoses, ships blowing their whistles and hundreds of small boats carrying "welcome home" signs. As the survivors headed for the dock, a band struck up a lively tune, and a great crowd surged forward amid popping flashbulbs and panning of TV cameras. When the excitement had died down, the commander received a letter from the Pan American captain. It read, in part, "I think you and your men are entitled to an unabashed feeling of deep pride as you contemplate your part in the episode."

Number Three

In 1980, the U.S. Coast Guard, assisted by the U.S. Air Force and the Royal Canadian Navy, rescued more than five hundred passengers and crew members from the cruise ship *Prinsendam* in the Gulf of Alaska.

The Coast Guard led one of the nation's largest search and rescue cases when the 519 passengers and crew members of the Dutch cruise liner *Prinsendam* were forced to abandon ship after a fire spread throughout the vessel. The *Prinsendam* was a 427-foot-long cruiser liner that was built in

1973. The ship was transiting through the Gulf of Alaska, approximately 120 miles south of Yakutat, Alaska, at midnight on October 4, 1980, when a fire broke out in the engine room.

Over the course of twenty-four hours, Coast Guard Cutters *Boutwell*, *Woodrush* and *Mellon*, as well as rescue aircraft deployed from Coast Guard Air Stations Sitka and Kodiak, would work side by side with the U.S. Air Force, Royal Canadian Navy and the AMVER-tasked tanker *Williamsburg* to rescue all hands from the sea. The rescue efforts were greatly complicated by twelve- to fifteen-foot-high seas and twenty-five- to thirty-knot winds generated by a nearby Arctic typhoon.

With conditions too dangerous for the deployment of small boats from the cutters, survivors were forced to climb aboard the tanker and cutters with the help of two Air Force pararescuemen, while hypothermic survivors were ferried to shore by rescue helicopters. The helicopters would then refuel and head back out to the scene for their next loads of passengers.

Within forty-eight hours, all survivors had been safely transferred to dry land, while the *Prinsendam* continued to burn. Despite the shipowner's efforts, *Prinsendam* finally rolled over and sank in heavy seas one week later.

In the immediate aftermath of the rescue, the Coast Guard identified areas of improvement in search and rescue operations, which would save tens of thousands of lives in the decades ahead. In the findings of the *Prinsendam* investigation, Rear Admiral Richard Knapp noted,

> *The training and expertise of the Air Force pararescuemen was responsible for the survival of passengers....It is notable that we were forced to rely on another agency to provide these personnel. I recommend we develop a similar, highly-trained, well-equipped rescue elite.*

Those "rescue elite" would, of course, become the Aviation Survival Technicians of the Coast Guard rescue swimmer program.

Another deficiency cited in the investigation was the need for rescue helicopters to return to shore to refuel while survivors remained in the water. The critical role rescue helicopters played during extended search and rescue cases would ultimately lead to helicopter in-flight refueling capability (allowing helicopters to refuel from ships while in a hover), which is now standard on Coast Guard rescue helicopters. The rescue of the *Prinsendam* was particularly significant because of the distance traveled by the rescuers, the coordination of independent organizations and the fact that all 519 passengers and crew were rescued without loss of life or serious injury.[23]

Number Two

On March 15, 1990, the Seattle-based ninety-six-foot-long crabber *Alaskan Monarch* lost power and became trapped in the ice-encrusted Bering Sea near St. Paul Island, Alaska. It was in danger of being swept onto the breakwater rocks outside St. Paul Harbor. Coast Guard Cutter *Storis* and an HH-3 helicopter from Air Station Kodiak, under the command of LT Laura H. Guth, responded. The *Alaskan Monarch* was en route to the St. Paul harbor to deliver 100,000 pounds of crab to Pribilof Island processors. As the *Alaskan Monarch* continued toward the harbor, it encountered an ice floe about one and a half miles from the harbor entrance. The *Alaskan Monarch* ran hard aground due to the dangerous rock bottom surrounding St. Paul Island. The *Monarch* and its crew were in peril.

Due to large amounts of heavy ice on the ocean's surface, there was only one Coast Guard Cutter in all of Alaska at the time that could take on such a challenge: the *Storis*. Due to its ⅛-inch-thick hull and proud history of cold weather service, the *Storis* was dispatched to help. It had served the

F/V Alaskan Monarch, Coast Guard Cutter *Storis* and Coast Guard HH-3F Pelican helicopter. *Photograph courtesy of Alaska State Library, coast guard collection.*

Coast Guard proudly off the coast of Greenland during World War II; it had also transited across the top of Canada in 1957 and had not slowed down, operating in brutal Alaskan waters for over thirty-three years.

Showing exceptional bravery by its crew, the *Storis* made several attempts to inch closer and closer to the grounded vessel in order to pass a heaving line to the *Monarch* and begin towing operations. The forty-eight-year-old *Storis* valiantly maneuvered the dangerous freezing waters and was on the cusp of running aground itself in order to save the small crew of the *Monarch*.[24]

As a backup, the Coast Guard also dispatched an HH-3 helicopter from Coast Guard Air Station Kodiak. Piloted by LT Laura Guth, the helicopter flew over six hundred miles, which included a winter crossing of the Alaska Peninsula and four hundred miles of frigid open water in a snowstorm. With the inability to pass a tow line to the *Monarch*, it was evident that the crew would have to be removed by helicopter.

Hoisting operations began, and four of the crewmen were rescued from the fo'c'sle (forecastle) before waves pushed the vessel hard onto the rocks. The vessel's captain and engineer left the wheelhouse and attempted to go

F/V Alaskan Monarch being swept by wave of brash ice. *Photograph courtesy of Alaska State Library, Coast Guard collection.*

forward and across the cargo deck. Halfway across, they lost their footing on the slippery deck and fell. Suddenly, a large wave of brash ice swept across the entire cargo deck, taking the captain and engineer overboard and into the ice-choked water.

Through precision helicopter maneuvers, challenged by limited remaining fuel, Guth and her crew rescued the two remaining crewmen from the water, saving them from certain death. She would later be awarded the Coast Guard Distinguished Flying Cross Medal for the rescue.

Number One

An overloaded Haitian vessel capsized alongside Coast Guard Cutter *Bear* in the Caribbean in 1992.

There have been several mass migrations from Cuba and Haiti over the years. Starting with the Mariel boatlift in 1980, which brought over 124,000 Cubans to the United States, migrant interdiction operations have demanded a substantial commitment of Coast Guard assets. The first exodus of Haitians followed the collapse of the Duvalier regime in the early 1980s, and a second took place after a military coup in 1991. In reality, from the Coast Guard perspective, these were massive search and rescue operations.

President Bush, in response to political and economic pressure, issued Executive Order 12807 in 1992, directing the secretary of transportation to issue appropriate instructions to the Coast Guard to enforce the suspension of the entry of undocumented aliens into the United States and to interdict the vessels carrying them. The Coast Guard mission transitioned from search and rescue to law enforcement operations. In practice, however, the interdiction operations remained as much humanitarian as they were law enforcement. Migrants typically took—and still take—great risks and endure significant hardships in their attempts to gain entry into the United States. In many cases, migrant vessels interdicted at sea are overloaded, unseaworthy, lack basic safety equipment and are operated by inexperienced seamen.[25]

History is replete with headlines of hundreds of migrants lost to the sea when overloaded vessels capsize or sink. Some of these incidents have high fatality rates because the rescue resources that are needed to address large numbers of people in the water are too distant to effectively respond. One incident, however, involved the rescue of 113 survivors in the shallow waters off the Turks and Caicos Islands.

While on migrant interdiction patrol in the Caribbean, the Coast Guard Cutter *Bear* encountered a severely overloaded Haitian migrant sailboat. As the *Bear*'s small boats maneuvered alongside in preparation for transferring the migrants to the cutter, migrants rushed to one side, capsizing the vessel and throwing many who were on board into the water. The *Bear*'s small boats responded by tossing life jackets to the people in the water and then recovering all without injury. This case demonstrated the danger that illegal migrants routinely put themselves in as they load unseaworthy, overcrowded boats in hopes of reaching the United States. The Coast Guard, while enforcing U.S. law, also ensures the safety of hundreds of illegal migrants annually as it intercepts these dangerous voyages.

In the period between 1980 and 2000, the Coast Guard rescued over 250,000 migrants from overcrowded, unseaworthy craft.

On December 27, 2000, the Coast Guard decided to reissue the "top ten" rescues that have been listed. However, one additional rescue was added and termed the "greatest rescue" of the century:

> Greatest Rescue: *Coast Guard Air Station Elizabeth City, North Carolina performs one of the most heroic and dramatic air-sea rescues in Coast Guard history.*[26]

It involved the flight of a HH-60 Jayhawk helicopter, Coast Guard 6031.

8

NO BANANAS

Nautical folklore is filled with a strange brew of legend and myth, sometimes developed from circumstance, often by mishap or tragedy. Sailors' superstitions might be well justified when they venture into the world of Poseidon and Neptune. A vessel's misfortune could result in a sailor's demise, and both would find their final resting place, a place known as Davy Jones's Locker.

To the dry-lander, it is hard to imagine the credence placed in various seagoing superstitions, but after months at sea in forbidding sailing conditions, with rations running low and suffering the ravages of scurvy, one can better understand the role of pleasing those who will protect you, calm the seas before you and guide you to safe harbor.

Until the late 1700s, sailing was an imperfect art. The inability to accurately determine longitude at sea, which requires accurate time to calculate, resulted in hundreds of shipwrecks and the loss of thousands of lives. Sailing in bad weather, dark nights or fog was risky business, and often, sailors and their captains would call for divine guidance.

In 1707, Britain suffered the catastrophic loss of four warships of a Royal Navy fleet in bad weather off the Isles of Scilly. Over 1,200 sailors perished due to a navigator's inability to get a fix of their longitude. The British Parliament would create a special committee to address the longitude problem and established a hefty reward to the one who could provide accurate time with a chronometer at sea. The committee sought the counsel of Sir Isaac Newton and Edmond Halley. It was over a half a century before Parliament paid their reward.

Those who went to sea knew of its danger and uncertainty, and superstitions would abound—and not just among the deckhands. All who sailed knew that it was smart not to invoke the wrath of King Neptune and that they could "hedge their bets" by avoiding bad omens. A multitude of superstitions have evolved over the ages that portend bad luck for a vessel or its crew. Bananas, for example, are thought to bring vessels bad luck, the origins of which are varied according to the raconteur. Ask a modern-day charter boat skipper about bringing bananas aboard, and you will get a quick and firm reply in the negative. A ship setting sail on a Friday was thought to invite bad luck. Most attribute the origins of this omen to Christ being crucified on a Friday.

Christening ceremonies were—and are—meant to bring good luck to new ships and those who sail on them. Christening new ships, or naming ceremonies, go back to the early days of sailing, and the ceremonies involved in naming and launching ships are based on traditions that are thousands of years old. In the early rituals, ship christenings by the Vikings were marked by the spilling of blood. In the Middle Ages, religious shrines were placed on ships, and a libation of wine was offered as the vessel hit the water as a substitute for the earlier blood sacrifice. The wine was poured on the deck to appease King Neptune and for good luck and a safe voyage. Ancient seafaring peoples rimming the Mediterranean launched their ships with rituals that had religious overtones. These practices, varying in form as nations and cultures evolved through the centuries, have carried over to the present christening and launching ceremonies. The current tradition throughout the world is that women christen ships, but it has not always been this way. Early ceremonies were performed by officials or local religious men.[27]

Superstition or not, the RMS *Titanic* was never christened. The White Star Line never used the practice in moving a new vessel from the ways to the water. The *Titanic* had two sister ships, RMS *Olympic* (mentioned earlier for slicing a U.S. lightship in two) and RMS *Britannic*. Although it would play an important role during World War I, by the end of its service, the *Olympic* would have two at-sea collisions and one inner-harbor collision. Like its sister ship *Titanic*, the *Britannic* would sail for less than a year. It experienced an explosion, possibly after hitting a mine, and sank in the Aegean Sea. Thirty lives were lost.

The USS *Arizona* was christened with a bottle of water rather than wine or champagne. The State of Arizona passed Prohibition in June 1915, five years before it became federal law. Many temperate Arizonans took a dim view to using champagne to christen a ship despite tradition. However, Navy men pointed out that christening a ship with water was an ill omen.[28]

Although rare, another ominous sign portending bad omens for a new ship is if it leaves the slipway at launching, rolls on its side or, even worse, capsizes and sinks. If it is righted, it will sail having that indelible history attached to its name.

Another remnant of nautical folklore that remains to this day is the renaming of a ship, which many still consider unlucky. *Exxon Valdez*, for example, was renamed *Exxon Mediterranean* after repairs and then had another change to *Sea River Mediterranean*. It was later sold and sailed under the new name *Don Fong Ocean*. In November 2010, it collided with the *Aali*, a cargo vessel in the South China Sea, and was damaged severely. Two years later, it was sold for scrap.

Built in 2001, the nine-hundred-foot-long container ship *Hanjin Cairo* sailed under its original name for five years. In November 2006, its name was changed to *Cosco Busan*. A year later, it allided with the San Francisco–Oakland Bay Bridge, spilling over fifty thousand gallons of heavy fuel oil into the bay.

The first name of the cruise ship *Achille Lauro* was *Willem Ruys*. In 1985, the *Achille Lauro* was hijacked by members of the Palestine Liberation Front. After that, it suffered a series of collisions and fires, and in 1994, it again caught fire and sank in the Indian Ocean.

The Royal Navy purchased the bulk cargo carrier *Bethia*. It was renamed HMS *Bounty*. On its last voyage, the crew attempted a westerly transit around Cape Horn. Conditions were forbidding, and after a month, it headed east, rounding Africa and moving into the Indian Ocean. Its mutinous crew would burn it to the waterline at Pitcairn Island.

Miss Penny was the first name of a commercial fishing vessel known to most as the *Andrea Gail*. In 1991, it was lost with all hands in what was termed "the perfect storm," which became the title of the book by Sebastian Junger and, later, a film.

In 1958, the cruise ship *Federico C.* was launched in Italy. It would sail under that name until 1983, when it became *Royale*. That same year, it became *StarShip Royale*. In 1988, it had another new name: *SeaBreeze I*. Its fate is part of this story.

9

A GRACEFUL GRAYING LADY

The Costa family had been involved in cargo shipping for over half a century when the founder's three sons, Federico, Enrico and Eugenio, decided to venture into the passenger vessel business. Most of their early passenger vessels had been purchased from other companies. The *Federico C.* was the first passenger vessel built for the shipping company. Launched in 1958, it was to be the flagship of the Costa passenger ship fleet. Unfortunately, it had an ominous beginning; the launching was a disaster. Once free of the slipway at the Ansaldo Sestri Ponente shipyard, it rolled over on its side, then completely capsized and soon sank in the harbor.

Bruce Nierenberg, the founder and former president and CEO of Premier Cruise Lines, knows the ship's history well.

> NIERENBERG. *It definitely happened at great embarrassment for the Costa Cruise Company. This was their first new ship after World War II. It was also named after the patriarch founder of the company, so it really was a huge boo-boo. Costa was a family-owned business at the time, and this was way before its sale to Carnival Cruise Lines in the late 1990s. I can't personally confirm the following, but since I was president of Costa in the early 1990s, I was told that the architect or someone at a high level of similar stature actually committed suicide after the ship launch was botched.*

Soon thereafter, *Federico C.* was refloated and outfitted to become a first-class passenger ship. At 605 feet long and twenty-one thousand tons of displacement, it had nine decks, and its two steam turbines could push it along at a respectable twenty-one knots. Initially, it cast an odd silhouette by today's cruise ship standards. The foreship resembled that of a mid-century freighter, with two sets of dual king posts, booms and derricks to facilitate over-the-rail cargo transfers. After a series of refits, the derricks disappeared, and it took on a graceful profile typical of contemporary cruise ships.

The *Federico C.* entered service in March 1958 as a passenger liner, connecting Genoa with Rio de Janeiro and Buenos Aires. Originally accommodating 1,200 passengers, it boasted newly developed innovative roll stabilizers, seven bars and four swimming pools. In eight years of service traversing this route, it carried three classes of passengers, including immigrants. In 1966, it began traveling from Italy to Florida, the Caribbean and Venezuela.

Following a refit in 1968, it began its "new" life as a cruise ship. Premier Cruise Lines purchased it in 1983, when it was again refitted and became the first ship in the new cruise line's fleet. It was renamed the *Royale*, and within a year, its name was changed again to *StarShip Royale*.

Bruce Nierenberg ran the original Premier Cruise Line along with his Norwegian partner, Bjornar Hermansen. The two men started the company in 1983 with the Greyhound-Dial conglomerate, which later became the Dial Corporation. For eight years, Premier Cruise Line operated a booming business driven by two advantages. First, after learning from marketing surveys that many cruise customers drove from central Florida to board ships in the Miami region, the new company decided to sail out of centrally located Port Canaveral. Second, rather than go after traditional cruise customers such as retirees and young couples, Premier targeted families with children. Market analysts would ask, "What do vacations, central Florida and families with children have in common?" The answer was obvious, Walt Disney World. So, Nierenberg brought costumed characters like Mickey Mouse and Donald Duck on short cruises to the Bahamas with stays at Disney World. Premier revolutionized the cruise industry. To secure its market share, Premier negotiated a deal to become the "Official Cruise Line of Walt Disney World."

Premier's most memorable marketing touch was the paint job. The original intent was to paint the line's first ship white—in the tradition of most cruise ships. Just to be sure, the company hired a Miami artist to render the ship in several colors. Meeting with Premier Executives, Fred Caravetta flipped through his acetate sketches. The response was ho-hum until he turned to a commanding image of a deep, rich red hull. Straightaway, everyone in the meeting knew red was it. The flashy paint job proved so unforgettable that it became a brand. As the company grew and acquired more ships, both Premier and its vessels became known as the "big red boats."[29]

Families packed the Big Red Boat from day one, and business grew throughout the 1980s. In 1986, Premier Cruise Line purchased its second ship from Home Lines, the classy vessel *Oceanic*, but when Nierenberg and Hermansen wanted to add more ships, the corporation told them they must first sell the original Big Red Boat. In 1989, Dolphin Cruise Line purchased the *StarShip Royale* from Premier and renamed it *SeaBreeze*.

Soon, other cruise lines would enter the "family cruise" business, and before long, the entire industry caught on and began catering to children. The coup de grace for Premier came in 1993, when Disney not only terminated its contract but also built two eighty-five-thousand-gross-ton cruise ships of its own.[30] So, with Dolphin Cruise Line, *SeaBreeze* was converted to a "one-class" ship, accommodating only 840 passengers. It served ports along the Eastern Seaboard, Caribbean and the Canadian Maritimes. Its passenger to crew ratio was almost two to one.

In 1997, Dolphin, Seawind and Premier would consolidate, but *SeaBreeze*, then long in the tooth, kept its name. However, in September 2000, all Premier ships were taken over by creditors and "arrested" in their last port of

Photograph courtesy of René Beauchamp.

call. On its way to Portland, Maine, the *SeaBreeze* reversed course to return to Halifax, Nova Scotia. *SeaBreeze* passengers were actually awakened by crew members and told to disembark in Halifax, halfway through their cruise. *SeaBreeze* would remain in Halifax with its captain, Solon Papadopoulos, and a skeleton crew. Its new owners planned to bring it to Charleston, South Carolina, with a stop in Boston for fuel and provisions. The transit was made without passengers but with a crew totaling thirty-four.

As is true for most large commercial ports in the United States, Boston Harbor has compulsory pilotage for ships that are entering or leaving harbor. On December 15, 2000, *SeaBreeze* entered Boston Harbor and anchored to wait for the stores barge and the fuel barge. After taking on fuel and stores, Captain Papadopoulos and the crew prepared for departure. They called for a harbor pilot to take them from anchorage to the pilot station near the harbor entrance sea buoy. The pilot was Captain Richard Stover.

> STOVER. *They called for a pilot to arrive at 2300. We arrived early, at about 2230, so I was asked to go to the captain's stateroom. I was informed the ship had no internal heating. When I got to the captain's cabin, I met the captain and first officer. They had a portable electric space heater in the cabin. We all huddled around the heater.*
>
> *After some casual discussion, we went to the bridge to get underway. I remember it was a cold December night, and the bridge had no heat, and her gyro compass was not operating.*
>
> *It was just before midnight on Friday that we weighed anchor and headed out of the harbor.*
>
> *At 0100 we reached the pilot station, and I disembarked onto the pilot boat.*

SeaBreeze sailed out of Boston Harbor on Friday, December 15. The local marine weather was a temperature of 33.1 degrees Fahrenheit, winds south–southwest at six miles per hour, ten miles of visibility, overcast skies and seas at one to two feet. It was the calm before the storm.

10
STORMY SEAS

History is full of tragic events at sea in which weather has sent many to a watery grave. Perhaps the most devastating singular event occurred during the Punic Wars, when the Romans had to battle not only the Carthaginians but also the weather. After defeating Carthage in one of many encounters, the Roman Navy found itself in a storm in the Mediterranean Sea, south of Sicily. Almost two-thirds of the Roman fleet was destroyed not by battle but by weather, and over 100,000 men were lost in the single storm. Historians estimate that more sailors were lost to weather at sea than actual combat between the Romans and Carthaginians.

We need not go to ancient history to find devastating loss of life due to weather at sea. In 1902, the *Camorta* was caught in a cyclone and sank in the Irrawaddy Delta of Myanmar, claiming the lives of 655 passengers and 82 crew members. In 1907, the passenger ship SS *Afrique* sank in the Bay of Biscay in bad weather. Almost 600 people died in the event. In 1912, more than 1,000 aboard the *Kiche Maru* died when the ship sank in a tropical storm in Southern Japan. In 1919, in the Gulf of Mexico, the steamship *Valbanera* sunk in a hurricane, claiming 488 lives. The Japanese passenger ferry *Toya Maru* sank in Typhoon Marie on September 26, 1954. Estimates are that almost 1,200 were lost in the event. In 1958, a Turkish-flagged ferry carrying about 280 people sank in heavy weather, taking the lives of all. The *Doña Marilyn* from Manila was caught in a typhoon in 1988, killing 389.

In more recent history, in 1993, the ferry *Seohae* from South Korea, which was carrying 362 passengers, sank in bad weather, claiming the lives of all on board. In 1994, the passenger ferry *Estonia* sank in heavy seas when the ship was crossing the Baltic Sea, from Tallinn, the capital of Estonia, to Stockholm, Sweden. It was carrying 989 people, 803 passengers and 186 crew members; 852 people were lost, and 137 survived. In 2000, an overloaded ferry from the Maluku Islands sank in a storm, claiming almost 500 lives. In November 2007, five ships sank in the Black Sea due to the weather conditions. The *Volgoneft*, *Nakhitchevan 139*, *Kovel* and *Volnogorsk*, all Russian-flagged cargo ships, and the *Hash Izmail*, a Georgian-flagged cargo ship, went down in the same storm.

Staggering casualties from adverse weather events are not limited to the open ocean. In 1913, a "cyclonic blizzard" struck the Great Lakes, and in a period of four days, twelve ships were sunk, claiming 255 lives. And we cannot forget the Great Lakes freighter SS *Edmund Fitzgerald* that sank in a Lake Superior storm in 1975, with the loss of the entire crew of 29. Its fate would later be recounted in a pop song by Gordon Lightfoot.

One of the most recent weather-related casualties close to home was the sinking of the SS *El Faro*. On Thursday, October 1, 2015, around 0715 Eastern Daylight Time, the Coast Guard received distress alerts from the 790-foot-long roll-on/roll-off container ship *El Faro*. The United States–flagged vessel, which was owned by TOTE Maritime Puerto Rico and operated by TOTE Services Inc., was forty miles northeast of Acklins and Crooked Island, Bahamas, and close to the eye of Hurricane Joaquin. The ship was en route from Jacksonville, Florida, to San Juan, Puerto Rico, with a cargo of containers and vehicles.

Just minutes before the distress alerts were received, the *El Faro* captain had called TOTE's designated person ashore and reported that a scuttle had

Photograph courtesy of Captain William Hoey.

popped open on deck no. 2 and that there was free communication of water into the no. 3 hold. He said the crew had controlled the ingress of water but that the ship was listing fifteen degrees and had lost propulsion. The Coast Guard and TOTE were unable to reestablish communication with the ship. Twenty-eight U.S. crew members, including an off-duty engineering officer who was sailing as a supernumerary, and five Polish workers were on board. All would perish.

The incident would be investigated by two federal agencies, the U.S. Coast Guard and the National Transportation Safety Board. The Coast Guard Marine Board of Investigation looks at marine casualties or accidents to document the casualties, uncover their causes and initiate necessary corrective actions. Specifically, it is responsible for evaluating all evidence to determine, as closely as possible:

- The cause of the accident.
- Whether there is evidence that any failure of material (either physical or design) was involved or contributed to the casualty so that proper recommendations for the prevention of the recurrence of similar casualties may be made.
- Whether there is evidence that any act of misconduct, inattention to duty, negligence or willful violation of the law on the part of any licensed or certified person contributed to the casualty so that appropriate proceedings against the license or certificate of such person can be taken.
- Whether there is evidence that any Coast Guard personnel or any representative or employee of any other government agency or any other person caused or contributed to the cause of the casualty.

At the completion of the investigation, the board prepared a report that contained findings of fact, causal analysis, conclusions and safety recommendations. The report was issued on September 24, 2017, and published as "STEAM SHIP *EL FARO*—MARINE BOARD'S REPORT 16732."

The Marine Board of Investigation identified a series of events and associated contributing factors *9.1.1. Event #1* EL FARO *Sailed Within Close Proximity to Hurricane Joaquin.* One of the conclusions affected the ship's captain:

9.1.1.11. The Master of EL FARO *failed to carry out his responsibilities and duties as Captain of the vessel between 800 p.m. on September 30 and 400 a.m. on October 1, 2015. Notably, the master failed to download the 1100 p.m. BVS (weather) data package and failed to act on reports from the 3/M [third mate] and 2/M [second mate] regarding the increased severity and narrowing of the closest point of approach to Hurricane Joaquin and the suggested course changes to the south to increase their distance from the hurricane.*[31]

The accident was also investigated by the National Transportation Safety Board. Among other things, it would look at the type and frequency of advisories issued by the National Hurricane Center (NHC), as well as the means of dissemination. On June 20, 2017, the NTSB issued a Safety Recommendation Report titled "Tropical Cyclone Information for Mariners." Specific findings were directed at the National Weather Service, NOAA and the U.S. Coast Guard. As part of the investigation, the NTSB provided a chilling account of the events early that morning

At 0120 EDT on October 1, the Second Mate called the Captain to suggest an alternative route, after which the second mate indicated to a helmsman that the Captain wished to stay on the planned route. About 10 minutes later, the NHC issued an intermediate public advisory (not received on board El Faro) indicating that Joaquin had moved southwest over the past 3 hours. That was about when El Faro completed a planned course change from 150 degrees true to 116 degrees true. At 0135 EDT, with El Faro heading 113 degrees true, Joaquin's center position, according to the just-issued intermediate public advisory, was 71 miles from El Faro, at 7 degrees to port.[32]

OVER TIME, SEVERAL FACTORS have improved safety at sea. Most important was the establishment of the International Maritime Organization (IMO) under the larger umbrella of the United Nations. Shipping is perhaps the most international of all the world's great industries—and it's one of the most dangerous. It has always been recognized that the best way to improve safety at sea is to develop international regulations that are followed by all shipping nations.

IMO's first task when it came into being in 1959 was to adopt a new version of the International Convention for the Safety of Life at Sea (SOLAS), the

A container ship leaving the Port of Hamburg. *Photograph by author.*

most important of all treaties dealing with maritime safety. Historically, the obligation of ships to go to the assistance of vessels in distress was enshrined both in tradition and, later, in the 1974 amendment to SOLAS, which states that the "master of a ship at sea which is in a position to be able to provide assistance, on receiving information from any source that persons are in distress at sea, is bound to proceed with all speed to their assistance, if possible, informing them or the search and rescue service that the ship is doing so."[33] Later, we will meet the masters of two merchant ships who honored this obligation in the worst of conditions.

But to specifically address hazardous weather at sea, the United States consolidated several agencies, including the National Weather Service, and formed the National Oceanic and Atmospheric Administration (NOAA) in 1970. The agencies that were brought together were among the oldest in the federal government; they included the United States Coast and Geodetic Survey, formed in 1807; the Weather Bureau, formed in 1870; and the Bureau of Commercial Fisheries, formed in 1871.

The Weather Bureau (later the National Weather Service) was established in 1870, when President Ulysses S. Grant signed a joint resolution of Congress authorizing the secretary of war to establish a national weather service. The original weather agency operated under the War Department from 1870 to 1891 with headquarters in Washington, D.C., and field offices concentrated mainly east of the Rocky Mountains. Little meteorological science was used to make weather forecasts during those early days. Instead, weather that occurred at one location was assumed to move into the next area downstream.

From 1891 to 1940, the Weather Bureau was part of the Department of Agriculture. The first two decades of the twentieth century had a remarkable effect on the nation's meteorological services. In 1902, the Weather Bureau's forecasts were sent via wireless telegraphy to ships at sea. In turn, the first wireless weather report was received from a ship at sea in 1905. Two years later, the daily exchange of weather observations with Russia and eastern Asia was begun.

The advent of computer technology in the 1950s paved the way for the formulation of complex mathematical weather models, resulting in a significant increase in forecast accuracy. Advances in weather satellites, radars, information processing and communication systems, automated weather observing systems and super computers provided for more timely and precise severe weather information.[34]

From the master mariner to the weekend angler in a small boat, weather is always the preeminent concern. While current, up-to-date weather forecasts are indispensable, there are other sources of general weather information to aid the shipping community and others who venture offshore.

The *American Practical Navigator*, first published in 1802, was billed as the "epitome of navigation" by its original author, Nathaniel Bowditch. The text has evolved with the advances in navigation practices since that first issue, and it continues to serve as a valuable reference for marine navigation in the modern day. The *American Practical Navigator* provides all mariners advice on route planning to address bad weather. It addresses a weather phenomenon known as the "extra-tropical" cyclone:

> *In the areas of the prevailing westerlies, migratory cyclones (lows) and anticyclones (highs) are a common occurrence. These are sometimes called extra-tropical cyclones and extra-tropical anticyclones to distinguish them from the more violent tropical cyclones. It should be noted that some extra-tropical cyclones do reach hurricane-force intensity.[35]*

In addition to providing marine weather forecasts for coastal areas and "blocks" of the ocean far offshore, the NOAA also publishes the Coast Pilot

Series, geographically specific publications that discuss general weather patterns. The geographical area for *Coast Pilot #2* is the Atlantic coast from Cape Cod, Massachusetts, to Sandy Hook, New Jersey. Among other things, it warns of the extra-tropical cyclone for this region.

> *Extra-tropical Cyclones, one of the biggest problems in these waters is the winter storm; the most powerful of these is the "Nor'easter." It generates rough seas, strong winds and high tides that threaten safety at sea and cause damage in port. These storms do not often come without warning. Approaching from the U.S. mainland or from the seas to the south, they are usually well forecasted. Difficulty arises when they develop or deepen explosively off the mid-Atlantic Coast. Sometimes called "Hatteras Storms," these lows can grow from small, weak frontal waves to full-blown systems in less than 24 hours. Not only can their circulation expand to cover most of the western North Atlantic, but they often accelerate rapidly northeastward. In the exposed waters, these storms can generate 40-foot (12 m) waves and hurricane-force winds. Each year, more than 40 extra-tropical systems move across or close to this coast. They average about two to four per month, but as many as ten can affect the region in a single month. Most systems are weak, but a few generate gales and rough seas for hundreds of miles, particularly from September through April.*[36]

NOAA provides updated weather forecasts for coastal and offshore areas in several formats: radio broadcasts, online interactive websites and email, by request. This was the weather forecast for December 17, 2000, that was available to the *SeaBreeze* and other vessels transiting the block of ocean known as ANZ085, about two hundred miles east of the Virginia coast:

Marine Weather Forecast—0939 EST

OFFSHORE WATERS FORECAST
NATIONAL WEATHER SERVICE, WASHINGTON, D.C.
MARINE PREDICTION CENTER/MARINE FORECAST BRANCH
9:30 A.M. EST SUN 17 DEC 2000
ANZ085-172030
BALTIMORE CANYON TO HATTERAS CANYON

...STORM WARNING...

THIS AFTERNOON...S WINDS 40 TO 50 KT BECOMING SW. SEAS 10 TO 14 FT BUILDING TO 14 TO 20 FT... HIGHEST NEAR 1000 FMS. SHOWERS AND TSTMS WITH VSBY BELOW 1 NM...ENDING FROM W TO E WITH VSBY IMPROVING.

TONIGHT...W WINDS DECREASING TO 25 TO 30 KT. SEAS SUBSIDING TO 10 TO 15 FT.

MONDAY...W TO NW WINDS DECREASING TO 10 TO 15 KT. SEAS SUBSIDING TO 4 TO 8 FT.

NOAA would update the weather forecast that afternoon.

Marine Weather Forecast—1500 EST

OFFSHORE WATERS FORECAST
NATIONAL WEATHER SERVICE, WASHINGTON, D.C.
MARINE PREDICTION CENTER/MARINE FORECAST BRANCH
3:00 P.M. EST SUN 17 DEC 2000
ANZ085-180330
BALTIMORE CANYON TO HATTERAS CANYON

GALE WARNING...

TONIGHT...W WINDS 35 TO 40 KT. SEAS 15 TO 20 FT.

The Nor'easter that strafed the mainland was forecast to move offshore, gain strength and grow into a full-blown gale, with thunderstorms, seas running from fifteen to twenty feet and sustained winds of fifty knots and gusting higher. Weather this bad is never welcome news to the mariner already at sea.

11

WRIGHT BROTHERS DAY

Sunday, December 17, 2000

A large Coast Guard Air Station can turn into a virtual ghost town on weekends and holidays. The typical weekend duty section consists of aircrews for the "ready" aircraft and minimal support staff. With the exception of base security, only a small staff works in operations and maintenance. For Coast Guard Air Station Elizabeth City, North Carolina, normal weekend readiness consists of one HH-60J Jayhawk helicopter aircrew, one HC-130 Hercules (fixed-wing) aircrew, the operations duty officer and a small aircraft support group for each aircraft type, typically less than ten people each.

Sunday, December 17, 2000, would be an exception. This day, one additional helicopter aircrew and one additional C-130 aircrew were present. Along with aircraft from other services, they were to participate in the annual Wright Brothers Day Flyover at the Kill Devil Hills Memorial, less than thirty-five air miles away. Rapidly deteriorating weather made the event look very doubtful. A strong Nor'easter was punishing the mid-Atlantic region of the Eastern Seaboard. General Ed Eberhart, United States Air Force, was en route to Coast Guard Air Station Elizabeth City to meet up with two Navy helicopters from Naval Air Station Oceana in Virginia Beach, Virginia. General Eberhart was slated to officiate for the Wright Brothers Memorial Ceremony. He and his wife were flying to the Air Station in a military C-37 (Gulfstream V). General Eberhart was piloting the Gulfstream. It was planned that, after landing at the Coast Guard Air Station, the general and his wife would transfer over to the Navy helicopter, which would take them the remaining distance to Kill Devil Hills.

0730

Commander Charlie Holman arrived at the Air Station. He was the oncoming watch relief as senior duty officer. If a search and rescue mission was to come in on his watch and require a response by a C-130, Holman was to be the pilot and on-scene commander. At the age of forty-five, he was, admittedly, quite old in the Coast Guard aviation community of pilots.

> HOLMAN. *At the time, I was serving on a two-year tour extension at Air Station Elizabeth City. I had previously submitted a retirement letter, but "pulled" my letter to extend active duty service to keep my 12-year-old son enrolled in TriCare healthcare; he was battling an orthopedic crippling disease, Legg Perthes Disease. Withdrawing my retirement letter committed me to two additional years, but it kept my son in his recovery program with his world-renowned primary orthopedic surgeon. It was a good move; it helped my son recover and my family endure this difficult time. Plus, I was able to help mariners get through this rough ordeal and return home.*
>
> *I was a department head at the Air Station, serving as the engineering officer. Even though Air Station department heads were not expected to stand duty…I did. I volunteered for standing SAR duty, and I enjoyed it. Plus, I could teach the younger pilots who were "moving up" in their aircraft qualifications.*

On account of the storm, Commander Holman had given himself extra time to get to work. It took an hour for him to drive from his house in Chesapeake, Virginia, to the Air Station in North Carolina.

> HOLMAN. *It was really nasty weather. Driving down, I was thinking, "This is not good."*

Commander Holman was aware that a high-ranking Air Force general was to arrive soon and wanted to make sure that every detail planned for his support at the Air Station was addressed. The brutal Nor'easter would complicate everything.

> HOLMAN. *I arrived early to ensure that all matters relating to USAF General Eberhart's flight arrival were complete prior to his arrival. General Eberhart was to land at 0830 to awaiting USN H-3 helicopters from Oceana, Virginia, for transport to Kitty Hawk, North Carolina, for*

the Wright Brothers ceremony and historic "Fly-By." The Navy H-3s canceled their departure due to weather. The weather at the time was 800 feet overcast, wind 180 at 25 knots with gusts to 35 knots. Visibility was 5 NM with heavy rain and lightning. The operations duty officer (ODO) LT Josh Fulcher had set the "Heavy Weather Bill" prior to watch relief. The Operations Center was working alternative ground transportation to take the General and his wife to Kitty Hawk. LT Dan Molthen was engaging the VIP/flag officer issues smartly.

0800

The roster for the helicopter-ready crew, often referred to as the "B Zero" crew, had Lieutenant Dan Molthen and Lieutenant Junior Grade Craig Neubecker flying together. Both were qualified aircraft commanders, but Coast Guard protocols dictate that the more senior officer is designated as the "Pilot in Command" and signs for the aircraft.

Tall and thin with a swimmer's physique, Molthen was balding prematurely, sporting an apron of black hair to the sides and back, cut short to meet military grooming standards. Having already received the Coast Guard Distinguished Flying Cross for a heroic rescue off of the Florida coast, he brought years of flying experience in challenging rescue operations. He had flown into danger before and spoke little of it—"Just part of the job."

Neubecker, the copilot, was a well-built, six-foot-two, blond-haired, blue-eyed Kansan with years of Army and Coast Guard flying experience. He was articulate and jovial most times, which were good personality traits to have, as his collateral duty was as the Air Station's public affairs officer. Newly married at the time, he had met his wife of a year, Kimberly, who was also in the Coast Guard, while he was in training, transitioning from the Army to the Coast Guard.

Joining the flight crew was flight mechanic Aviation Maintenance Technician Second Class Lorne Green and rescue swimmer Aviation Survival Technician First Class Darren Reeves. Reeves was a buffed-out forty-year-old of average height. He was old by today's standards to sustain the rigors and physical demands of a Coast Guard rescue swimmer, but his lack of youth was made up for by his years of experience. With thinning hair in front, he was soft-spoken but deliberate in conversation. He knew and practiced his art well, never keeping count of the many lives he had already saved. Lorne Green was quiet and soft-spoken, deliberately focused at work. He was a veteran of dozens of rescue missions and a key player during hoisting operations. Not just part of a team, the flight mechanic is a critical player in both directing the helicopter and supporting the rescue swimmer from above. In the event of a SAR mission, AMT2 Green would be the hoist operator, and AST1 Reeves would be deployed from the helicopter.

The flight crew was assigned the ready helicopter, CG 6031, and conducted their aircraft mandatory preflight inspection, part of the routine on arrival. The ready helicopter was already configured with two external fuel tanks. A third external tank could be added if a mission required extra fuel.

The roster for the C-130 ready crew had Commander Charlie Holman flying with copilot Lieutenant Eric Storch. The crew was completed with a flight engineer, navigator, radio operator, basic air crewman, a loadmaster and a drop master for deployable equipment. The loadmaster and drop master also serve as search "scanners." In the event of a SAR mission, they would fly CG 1504, the ready aircraft.

Flight Engineer AMT2 Don Welch
Navigator AVT1 Sean Fuller
Radio Operator AVT3 Omar Acuna
Drop-Master AMT3 Eric Benson
Load-Master AMT1 Ed Vickrey

Despite the weather, the second helicopter aircrew and C-130 aircrew were making preparations for the flyover of the Wright Brothers Memorial site at Kill Devil Hills. They were not part of the ready crew duty section, but they were actively performing preflight checks for the flight. The helicopter flyover crew included Lieutenant Commander Randy Watson and copilot Ensign Steve Bonn. Watson was a veteran of several challenging rescues that eventually got him the Coast Guard Distinguished Flying Cross Medal. He cast a tall shadow. Outwardly stoic, he was reluctant to talk about himself, moving discussion instead to the teams he flew with.

His copilot, Steve Bonn was a newbie to the Coast Guard but brought years of flying experience from duty with the Army. A Kevin Bacon look-alike, he was outgoing and professional, anxious to fit in with his new Coast Guard family. Their flight mechanic was Avionics Electrical Technician Second Class (AET2) Samuel Pulliam.

Because the flyover was not a SAR mission, there was no rescue swimmer assigned to the crew. The helicopter that was to be used for the event was

CG 6001. This helicopter also had only two external fuel tanks attached, more than enough fuel to accomplish the flyover that was only thirty-five miles away. The assigned C-130 aircrew for the flyover had Lieutenant Commander John Keeton as the aircraft commander and Lieutenant Kristina "Tina" Ahmann as the copilot. The designated aircraft had the tail number CG 1500; it was the oldest C-130 that was still flying with the Coast Guard at the time.

After the preflight routines were complete, some of the ready crew spent their time working on their assigned collateral duties; some hunkered down in the Officer's Wardroom or ready room for a day of football. The Buffalo Bills were playing the New England Patriots with a start time of 1300—it was a game they would not see.

LT Molthen had other ideas.

0810

Watch relief had been accomplished. Commander Holman continued to work on the general's arrival. Given the horrible weather conditions, Holman had considered the possibility of canceling all previously scheduled nonessential Coast Guard flights.

General Eberhart was orbiting the Air Station, looking for a break in the weather to make a safe landing. It did not happen.

0820

Holman briefed the Air Station's commanding officer Captain Bob Odom and Operations Officer Commander Joe Seebald by telephone, saying that since the Navy helicopters from NAS Oceana had been scrubbed due to adverse weather, the Air Force general would probably have to land at Elizabeth City and wait for alternate ground transportation.

> HOLMAN. *I directed quick check and clean-up of the wardroom to accept the general; (LT Storch accomplished graciously). The ODO and LT Molthen were working with the USAF for ground transportation for the general.*

0825

Due to the increasingly deteriorating local weather, General Eberhart opted to not land at the Air Station and canceled his scheduled appearance at Kill Devil Hills. He and his aircrew turned back to his command in Colorado. All Coast Guard support efforts were terminated.

CDR Holman again checked the weather for the entire Eastern Seaboard to determine whether the other scheduled flight missions should be scrubbed.

0830

Due to the wind conditions at Elizabeth City and the weather offshore, the Fifth Coast Guard District C-130 law enforcement mission was canceled. The weather system, which had left a trail of killer tornadoes in Alabama, passed over the Air Station at 0745 and moved offshore. At the heart of the gale, two lines of thunderstorms lit up the weather radar with bright red cells. The squall lines were sweeping northeast across the Outer Banks and over the open ocean. The weather radar showed two extensive weather systems with heavy precipitation and system cloud tops at forty-five thousand feet.

Commander Holman proceeded to C-130 Maintenance Control to check the aircraft maintenance records for CG 1504, the ready aircraft.

0930

Given the adverse weather that was battering the Eastern Seaboard, the "fly by" pilots consulted with each other about the risks of flying in such bad weather, only to participate in the Wright Brothers event. They decided to commit one helicopter, but the C-130 that was initially planned for the event would stay grounded. Ten minutes later, CG 6001 took off for the short flight to Kill Devil Hills. Ensign Bonn recalled the event.

> BONN. *Randy* [Watson] *and I were only there that day to do a flyover at the Wright Brothers Memorial for the ceremony, so they didn't have to commit the duty crew to do it. Even though the weather was too bad for the larger fixed-wing aircraft to be able to fly, we did make it down there with our helicopter. It was cloudy and raining.*

1000

Even though the main weather front had already passed, thunderstorms, lightning and gale-force winds were predicted for the next several hours. Around midmorning, the feed from the television satellite dish stopped, and the television screen turned to snow. Seasoned watch standers saw this as a bad omen. By myth or actual experience, when one loses satellite TV, a SAR mission will soon follow.

Having attended to all required checks for the duty crew coming on watch, Molthen went to rest in the ready crew berthing area. He was on duty for that weekend after swapping shifts when a buddy had visited earlier in the week. That day, he was tired. Friends who were at a Christmas party in Alaska had called him at 0300 that morning and kept him up for nearly two hours.

1115

Watson and Bonn returned from Kill Devil Hills to Coast Guard Air Station Elizabeth City and began to button up their helicopter.

1125

LTJG Neubecker received a call from his wife. As is customary on weekend duty, spouses may come aboard the base to bring lunch. His wife, Kim, was giving him options for the lunch menu. They did not finish their conversation.

1129

Communication Station (COMSAT) Southbury, Connecticut, received a satellite telephone distress call from the captain of the *SeaBreeze* Solon Papadopoulos. COMSAT Southbury relayed the call to the Fifth Coast Guard District Rescue Coordination Center (RCC), Portsmouth, Virginia.

LCDR Mark Rizzo heard the call come in.

> RIZZO. *We could tell by the distress in their voices that it was an emergency situation.*

In response to Captain Papadopoulos's distress call, the Coast Guard Rescue Coordination Center (RCC) replied:

RCC. *Sir, this is the U.S. Coast Guard. What is the name of your vessel?*

The captain shouted his response to each question, hoping to eliminate any misinterpretation.

Papadopoulos. SeaBreeze One, SeaBreeze One.

RCC. *What is the state of your vessel? Will it be able to stay afloat?*

Papadopoulos. *We lost engine…listing. Listing now. Listing. Send help, please.*

RCC. *How many people onboard?*

Papadopoulos. *Thirty-four people. Thirty-four people.*

There was a momentary break in radio communications. Nothing was said. Papadopoulos broke the silence: "Send helicopter!"

Captain Papadopoulos reported that the *SeaBreeze* was taking on water and listing severely in heavy seas. He stated that the *SeaBreeze* was a six-hundred-foot-long cruise ship with a skeleton crew of thirty-four aboard and approximately two hundred miles offshore of Norfolk, Virginia. He further reported that only one engine was operational and providing only limited power. Only thirty minutes remained until electrical power would be lost. The flooding below decks was uncontained. He stated that once power was lost, the crew would abandon ship. The captain had the intention of putting survivors into two inflatable life rafts. An emergency position indicating reporting beacon (EPIRB) would be with the life rafts once deployed.

LT Jason Ryan, RCC Duty Officer, telephoned the Operations Duty Officer LT Josh Fulcher at Coast Guard Air Station Elizabeth City to initiate a response. RCC called Vice Admiral John Shkor, the Commander of Coast Guard Atlantic Area and Fifth Coast Guard District, at home to brief him on the mission. VADM Shkor canceled his afternoon schedule and headed into the Coast Guard Operations Center in Portsmouth, Virginia, to monitor radio traffic.

1130

The SAR alarm sounded throughout Coast Guard Air Station Elizabeth City. The Duty Officer called Commander Joe Seebald, the Operations Officer, at home. Seebald replied that he would come into the Air Station. Before leaving home, Seebald called Captain Bob Odom, the commanding officer of Coast Guard Air Station Elizabeth City. Captain Odom and his wife, Natalie, were at church. Odom left church and went home to change into his uniform. He then drove to the Air Station.

Commander Holman grabbed the Air Station intercom to assemble the duty SAR crew. After describing the SAR case, location of the vessel and the impending weather, Holman added a comment:

> HOLMAN. *The Coast Guard is going to make headlines today, and it isn't going to be pretty.*

The search and rescue alarm jolted Molthen from a dead sleep. He jumped up, thinking, "What? A cruise ship is sinking?"

Even though it was a Sunday, the Air Station Executive Officer Commander Rod Ansley was in his office doing officer evaluation reports, administrative paperwork with firm deadlines. CDR Ansley was copilot-qualified on the HH-60 Jayhawk. He heard the SAR alarm and walked across the alleyway to the OPCEN to say that he was aboard and, if they need another helicopter pilot, he was available.

The duty section dropped everything and moved into action. Once plotted on a chart, the flight crews found the reported position of the *SeaBreeze* to be 236 nautical miles offshore, the very outer limits of their range. Preflight checks included an updated weather report. The offshore weather was going from bad to horrible.

SPC MESOSCALE DISCUSSION #2113 FOR DE...MD...NC...
NJ...PA...VA...CW
CONCERNING...SEVERE THUNDERSTORM POTENTIAL...
REF WW821...

SEVERAL CONFLUENT ZONES EXIST ACROSS THE MID-
ATLANTIC REGION AHEAD OF MAIN SYNOPTIC COLD
FRONT ADVANCING EWD ALONG THE CREST OF THE
APPALACHIAN MOUNTAINS. IT APPEARS THAT STORMS

ARE BEGINNING TO INTENSIFY ALONG ONE SUCH ZONE SITUATED FROM 25 N ILG-NHK-ORF (Norfolk, VA) VICINITY.

AIRMASS AHEAD OF THIS BOUNDARY REMAINS UNSTABLE, WITH UNSEASONABLY WARM DEW POINTS IN THE 60S UNDERNEATH MIDLEVEL LAPSE RATES OF 7-7.5 C/KM...CONTRIBUTING TO MUCAPES TO 2500 J/ KG. AMBIENT WIND REGIME REMAINS VERY STRONG, AND REGIONAL VWP DATA SUGGEST 40–60 KT SWLY WINDS JUST OFF THE SURFACE AND SUFFICIENT DEEP LAYER SHEAR FOR POSSIBLE ROTATING UPDRAFTS. AS THIS BOUNDARY ADVANCES EWD THROUGH WW... INDIVIDUAL STORMS WILL TEND TO BOW GIVEN FAIRLY UNIDIRECTIONAL FLOW. HOWEVER...THE THREAT FOR ISOLATED TORNADOES WILL REMAIN, ESPECIALLY WHERE THE LOW LEVEL FLOW IS BACKED AHEAD OF THE LINE OVER SRN NJ...DE AND THE LOWER SHORES OF ERN MD.

A forecast of "severe thunderstorm potential" with the possibility of tornadoes is exactly the type of weather to be avoided. Flying in such conditions would present clear danger to the aircrews and their aircraft. Pilots have various terms for flying in very bad weather and zero visibility.

NEUBECKER. *Some pilots describe solid instrument meteorological conditions (IMC) where there is no visibility as flying in the goo, the muck, or the crud. But when you add hurricane-force winds, severe turbulence, and squall lines with lightning all around, the weather conditions could only be described as horrific.*

Watson, Bonn and Pulliam completed their postflight chores and were about to leave for home to enjoy the remainder of the weekend.

BONN. *We had completed the* [Wright Brothers Memorial] *flyover, had changed out of our uniforms and were literally about two minutes from walking out the door to go home. Just then, the Operations Duty Officer stuck his head out the doorway just down the hall and yelled to us, "Guys, don't leave yet! We might need you!" That was the first notice we got. We didn't know what was going on just yet.*

Since the "flyover" helicopter was not initially designated for a search and rescue mission, the aircrew had no assigned rescue swimmer. Darren Reeves called his close friend AST3 Robert Florisi at home.

> REEVES. *Bobby, get in here. This is a big one.*

Florisi, tall and physically attuned to meet the challenges of being a Coast Guard rescue swimmer, was a fun and outgoing Texan who loved his work. Even though he was not scheduled for duty, he arrived at the Air Station in less than fifteen minutes.

The helicopter crews quickly donned dry suits and proceeded to their assigned aircraft.

> BONN. *We wore our dry suits for the flight. It is standard procedure for almost every flight that time of year. Coast Guard policy is that when we will be over water and the water temp is less than seventy degrees Fahrenheit, we must wear the suits.*

The distance offshore is no problem for the C-130, but at 236 nautical miles, the crew of helicopter CG 6031 had to strap on an additional 120-gallon external fuel tank, giving the aircraft all of the fuel it could hold.

To provide maximum space inside the helicopter cabin, the flight crews of both helicopters decided not to take their large cooler with their sodas and box lunches. They also removed the dewatering pumps, litters and other nonessential gear to make more room in the cabin. An anticipated load of seventeen rescuees each would exceed a previous record for the H-60 Jayhawk of thirteen; they would need all the room they had. The cooler and their food would stay at the Air Station for their return.

The C-130 aircrew scrambled to the flight line, entered the plane to quickly light off the four Allison T56-A-15 turboprops, each having 4,590 shaft horsepower. With cockpit checklists complete, Commander Holman taxied CG 1504 to the runway.

1200

At exactly noon, CG 1504, piloted by CDR Charlie Holman and copilot LT Eric Storch, lifted off the runway at Elizabeth City and turned toward the *SeaBreeze*, which was over 236NM (272 statute miles) away. LT Molthen had already lifted CG 6031 into a hover to perform hover checks to make sure they would not only have the hover power to complete the mission but also that all systems and flight instruments were working properly. At the same time, AMT2 Greene was busy in the helicopter's cabin completing the mandatory rescue checklist to ensure that all the needed rescue equipment was on board and in working order for the mission. With the hover and rescue checklists completed, CG 6031 followed CG 1504 into the dark skies and thunderstorms that lay ahead.

> STORCH. *This was one of the rare instances we got ahead of the H-60 we are escorting. We typically take longer to get airborne and lag behind but are able to catch up due to our much faster cruise speed.*
>
> *We took off to the west, and immediately upon reaching four hundred feet off the departure end of runway 28, Charlie [Holman] told me to bank sharply to the north, so I abruptly dropped the right wing to forty-five degrees angle of bank to expedite our turn offshore, direct to the last-known position of* SeaBreeze. *My wife, Laurie, was outside at the time, and our ground track brought us directly over the neighborhood. She later told me that she knew instantly that we were launched on something big where time was of the essence because we typically don't make low-level turns at such high angles of bank.*

Even though the engines were still warm from the flyover event, the crew of the second helicopter, CG 6001, scrambled to get the helicopter ready for the long flight.

> BONN. *We did have to preflight, which is normal anytime we fly anything, just to give a good once-over again. We also did take the time to strap on the additional external fuel tank due to the distance we would be flying. This also worked well into our timing for take-off. Since the report said that there were thirty-four crewmembers aboard, we discussed the initial plan on how to get all of them with Dan and Craig. Not knowing if we would even be able to launch a third helicopter, we decided that we would each plan to hoist seventeen people, if possible.*
>
> *Randy and I planned to take off thirty minutes after 6031 so we wouldn't waste time burning valuable fuel just loitering around waiting for the other helo to conduct their hoists if we both got out there at the same time. This would hopefully be the right amount of time for them to complete their hoists before we arrived on scene.*

⌁

COMMANDER HOLMAN BECAME THE on-scene commander, and the C-130 then used the call sign "Rescue 1504."

> HOLMAN. *This gives us certain priorities when flying. Air traffic control centers do their best to accommodate our requests when we use the "Rescue" call sign. It also helps when we enter the ADIZ (Air Defense Identification Zone) when we are far offshore. They know who we are and don't have to run an intercept on us.*

The flight crew "punched in" the LAT-LONG (latitude and longitude coordinates) of the ship's last-reported position into the inertial navigation system. This flight would almost entirely rely on instrument navigation until finding the *SeaBreeze*. The C-130 would find *SeaBreeze*, and it would also provide communications support and crucial local weather advisories to the following aircraft. The weather worsened.

> HOLMAN. *Shortly upon crossing the North Carolina shoreline, we were able to climb to four thousand feet to search for less turbulent air. We checked in with Oceana Approach Control and informed them of the pending case and expected rescue air traffic to follow. I switched to "Giant Killer" radio frequency and informed radar controllers of the case and of the aircraft involved and operational area we were proceeding to. I inquired about air space warning areas. We requested radar flight following and coordination with air defense radar for the return flights.*
>
> *Approximately twenty NM offshore, CG 1504 encountered moderate to severe turbulence and slowed to penetration speed of 180 KTS; I directed crew to secure loose items and check that safety belts are secure. CG 1504 was unable to maintain reference with the surface and climbed in instrument conditions.*
>
> *The Air Station ODO was relaying weather conditions, both en route and on scene via UHF radio. Utilizing the pilot's APN-215 weather radar in combination with the navigator's APS-137 radar, CG 1504 continued to navigate through continuous moderate with occasional severe turbulence and heavy precipitation en route to the scene.*

Several times, the C-130 deviated from their chosen course to avoid severe weather. Even with this effort, they experienced severe turbulence, incessant lightning and zero visibility. At one point, the turbulence became so severe that three of the seasoned aircrew got airsick.

> HOLMAN. *These crew members were in the aft section of the aircraft. I asked them to come up front so they could see outside. They just had to hang on due to the turbulence. Being able to look out ahead helped with the air sickness.*

Although finding *SeaBreeze* was the main objective, Holman's biggest concern was flying in such horrific weather.

> HOLMAN. *In order to reach the SeaBreeze, we penetrated two separate and distinct squall lines, which, at times, caused the aircraft to execute uncommanded climbs, and descents, and roll twenty degrees from a wings-level attitude with no pilot input.*
>
> *Proceeding to the vessel, we were using radar to dodge convective build-ups; we eventually found ourselves headed 180 degrees from our original course, so we decided to press on directly to the vessel's last-known position and only deviate when the lightning was severe.*
>
> *I tried climbing and descending to avoid the severe weather associated with the weather front/system. I finally opted to position the aircraft below the weather to proceed to SeaBreeze and track our helicopters' progress.*

The severe turbulence persisted. LT Storch would later comment that this flight was the only time in his flying career that he ever locked his restraint harness. Commander Holman described the turbulence differently.

> HOLMAN. *In very severe turbulence like this, the instrument panel shakes so violently that the instruments become unreadable. It was that bad.*
>
> *I mentioned to LT Eric Storch that if he flew for a career in the Coast Guard, there will be four or five missions where you will fly in the worst weather imaginable. You will remember these flights. You will tell the young pilots that you train, that the C-130 aircraft can take a tremendous beating; it was designed to do so. Flights like this test your capabilities and take you to the edge of your own and the aircraft's limitations…all can be accomplished safely.*

About thirty minutes into the flight, in one of the prolonged violent shaking episodes, a critical avionics component failed. The traffic collision avoidance system (TCAS), which was used to keep safe separation of aircraft in a confined area, went down and stayed down. It presented serious safety concerns to the aircrew, as they knew that they could soon be flying in a confined area, in bad weather and close to rescue helicopters.

> HOLMAN. *Yeah, the TCAS helps us avoid the helicopters, especially* [when] *flying in reduced visibility or zero vis. It also allows us to track the helicopters' location and progress to the search area. This was a real problem. We started using TACAN to maintain aircraft separation.*[37]

1215

The Commanding Officer Captain Bob Odom and the Operations Officer Commander Joe Seebald wanted a third helicopter airborne "as a safety net." The Air Station had only three helicopters assigned, and the third helicopter, CG 6026, was in Charlie status (down for maintenance), not slated for service or expected to be operational. It was to be a "heavy lift" for the small weekend duty maintenance crew to get the helicopter flyable, but they accepted the challenge knowing that lives may have been at stake.

Further complicating matters and adding to the maintenance issue with the remaining helicopter was the fact that there was no aircrew. Odom, Seebald and Fulcher scrambled to get another aircrew not knowing if the helicopter was even going to be operational. The Air Station Executive Officer Commander Rod Ansley, already at the Air Station, was told that he was needed. He was to fly as copilot. They still needed a pilot, flight mechanic and rescue swimmer. Calls were hurriedly made to off-duty personnel in a fervent attempt to fill the gaps. They would find their people.

1225

Unable to find clear skies and smooth air between four thousand and seven thousand feet, Rescue 1504 initiated a descent to one thousand feet over the water and continued offshore through turbulence, dark skies and lightning. Once they were clear of the squall lines, they increased airspeed and headed directly for the *SeaBreeze*. The aircraft was depressurized, and smoke flares were loaded in the flare launch tubes to assist in locating people in the water. Rafts were readied to address the possibility of large numbers of people in the water, possibly scattered by the wind and waves. Strobe lights and sea dye markers were attached to MK-25 smoke flares to mark water targets should sea conditions have hindered the relocation of the smoke and flares.

1239

The helicopter crew of CG 6001, having already flown to Kill Devil Hills, had added an additional fuel tank and a rescue swimmer, AST3 Robert Florisi. They departed Coast Guard Air Station Elizabeth City and headed east into the blackened skies. This was the first rescue for Ensign Steve Bonn.

1245

The radio operator aboard Rescue 1504 made a call on VHF-FM Channel 16, the international maritime distress frequency, for any vessels in the area to assist in the rescue effort and, if necessary, provide an emergency landing pad for rescue helicopters. There was no response. A minute later, a surface target was spotted on the weather radar system. It was an eight-hundred-foot-long vessel approximately thirty-five nautical miles from the *SeaBreeze*. Rescue 1504 attempted radio communication; again, there was no response. Holman changed course and headed for the radar target.

Suddenly, there was a response on channel 16 but not from the radar contact. Captain Solon Papadopoulos, who was aboard the *SeaBreeze* heard the radio call from Rescue 1504 and intervened. CDR Holman explained that he was attempting to divert a nearby ship and would soon be overhead orchestrating the rescue of the *SeaBreeze* crewmen.

Captain Papadopoulos reported that *SeaBreeze* was still afloat, listing and with limited power. The crew attempted to inflate two large life rafts to leave the ship, but both rafts were ripped from the crew by hurricane-force winds and were blown off *SeaBreeze*, tumbling over wave tops downwind.

Another attempt by Rescue 1504 to reach the radar target on channel 16 went without success.

1251

The duty maintenance crew performed miracles, and the third helicopter, CG 6026, was then fully fueled and ready to fly. The hastily called air crew, including LT Mark Ward, pilot; CDR Rod Ansley, copilot; a flight mechanic; and a rescue swimmer, were airborne and heading east, into the goo.

1254

Rescue 1504 intercepted the surface target and flew over its bow at an altitude of only two hundred feet. Communications were quickly established with the target vessel, M/V *Front Rider*. They asked it to divert, if possible, to the last-known position of *SeaBreeze*. M/V *Front Rider*, a large cargo vessel, reported that it was "helo deck capable," and its position was relayed to both rescue helicopters as an "emergency divert platform." The master of M/V *Front Rider* complied with the request but stated that, with the current sea conditions, the estimated time of arrival at the *SeaBreeze*'s last-reported position would be five to six hours.

Using the automated mutual-assistance vessel rescue system (AMVER), the Fifth Coast Guard District Rescue Coordination Center had already located other vessels in reasonable proximity of the *SeaBreeze*'s reported position and diverted them to assist.

Two of these vessels were under U.S. Navy command. The USS *Ashland*, a 610-foot-long dock landing ship with a helicopter capability was released from Commander Amphibious Squadron 4 to assist in the case. The USS *Saipan*, an 820-foot-long amphibious assault ship and the pride of the Gator Navy, was a virtual floating island, with a flight deck spanning just over 800 feet. Although it was over one hundred miles away, it was diverted to intercept the helicopters' return route to the mainland and offer assistance if the rescue helicopters experienced an emergency. Its call sign was "War Ship 2." Internal Coast Guard messaging explained that *Saipan* would "act as a lily pad for Air Station Elizabeth City aircraft and possibly provide additional SAR HELOS." It secured from underway replenishment operations and proceeded north at the best possible speed.

Within the hour, USS *Ashland* was released, but all the other vessels were proceeding to their assigned destinations in very heavy seas.

Rescue 6031 proceeded to the last-reported position of the *SeaBreeze* at an altitude of three hundred feet. Rescue swimmer Reeves had great concerns.

> REEVES. *We did not have good information about the condition of the ship and initially thought that there were people in the water.*

He did a mental calculation of the time required to rescue thirty-four people in the water and quickly realized that the helicopter did not have enough hover time (fuel) to rescue more than a handful. He envisioned the worst-case scenario that, even with two helicopters, some would be left behind.

Among the prolonged sessions of severe turbulence and relentless lightning, Reeves got glimpses of the sea below. He would later comment about the sea conditions.

> REEVES. *I was thinking, "We're this far out. The waves are this big. And we've got that many people in the water. If you do the math, I'm not coming back. You can't possibly hoist that amount of people out of those size waves in that amount of time." So, the thought went through my mind, "This may very well be it for me." So, I was scared, very scared. My mouth got dry.*

Reeves said so on the ICS.[38]

"I'm scared."

"Yeah," Molthen responded. "We're all scared!"

"No," Reeves thought. "That's not what I mean. I'm scared."

> REEVES. *I could barely mouth the words; my mouth was so dry. I really wanted to curl up in the fetal position in the back and say, "No, we're not going." I've been swimming in large waves before, thirty-foot waves, but nothing like this. I was flat-out terrified.*
>
> *You see conditions like that, and it makes you wonder if this is it. You actually might not come back. You know the old Coast Guard saying, "You have to go out, but you don't have to come back." Then you realize that it's your job, this is what you do. It's the anticipation that eats at you.*

Molthen recalled that the large waves would build to a height that caught the wind, and the tops of the waves would be totally sheared off.

The helicopter pilots were very concerned about flying through the unrelenting lightning and severe turbulence.

NEUBECKER. *The weather was certainly giving us all we could handle. We had severe turbulence and lightning everywhere around us—not good. Even flying at just two hundred to three hundred feet above the water, we were in the clouds and flying blind and, therefore, relying solely on the flight instruments to navigate us to the scene. Dan and I were really concerned up front because a lightning strike could knock out our radar, GPS and other avionics we were using to navigate to the* SeaBreeze. *A lightning strike would probably also knock out the electric fuel transfer pumps required to move the fuel in the three 120-gallon external tanks into the main internal fuel cells so it could be burned by the engines. If we lost those pumps, we would not have the range required to make it to the* SeaBreeze *and/or back to shore. Worst case, a lightning strike might even cause our engines to flame out, forcing us to auto rotate into the ocean below. So, between navigating us by radar and attempting to zig-zag us through the worst parts of the storm, manually transferring the fuel, communicating with the other aircraft and backing Dan up on the flight instruments, I was doing a lot of silent praying. Thank God the Lord was listening, as nothing really bad came to pass.*

1303

Having successfully diverted *Front Rider*, Rescue 1504 made a beeline to *SeaBreeze*'s reported position. Holman again contacted *SeaBreeze*'s bridge on channel 16, telling Papadopoulos that they were en route. Two minutes later, Rescue 1504 arrived on the scene and flew over *SeaBreeze* at an altitude of less than five hundred feet. They reported its position 37.39 N, 71.35 W.

Holman also reported that the *SeaBreeze* was still afloat but listing fifteen to twenty degrees to port, wallowing in the troughs of thirty- to fifty-foot-high swells. The "scanners" on board CG 1504 reported a black life raft being windswept and tumbling over wave crests in the heavy seas. They realized that this was one of the rafts that the *SeaBreeze* captain reported earlier.

HOLMAN. *Once I established communications with M/V* SeaBreeze, *they stated that they had minimum time afloat and were sinking. We asked the master if dewatering pumps would help him. The master stated that flooding was not contained; bilge pumps were unable to stop below-deck flooding. The master stated he had two people in the engine room keeping generators going for electrical power.*

On-scene weather conditions were challenging. Skies 500-700 overcast, winds south/southwest at 50 KTS, gusting to 70 KTS, visibility 4 NM, seas twenty-five feet, swells to thirty-five feet. SeaBreeze *was listing to port, steaming 1-2 KTS, heading 240 degrees magnetic.*

Lifeboats were deployed but still attached to port and starboard davits twenty feet from surface. The drop master on CG 1504 sighted two life rafts within 1 NM of SeaBreeze. *Smoke flares were deployed over rafts. One raft was orange; one was black; both [were] wind driven. The ship's position was passed to Rescue 6031.*

I confirmed thirty-four people on board SeaBreeze *by the master of the vessel. I confirmed that the life rafts were empty; the rafts were deployed in windy conditions that precluded boarding survivors and broke free. I briefed the master and prepped the vessel for immediate H-60 hoist Operations. We identified the stern area for hoist operations; I provided the standard Coast Guard helo hoist brief; I requested that all people on board don personal floatation devices. I briefed the master that the Coast Guard rescue swimmer (from the helo) would deploy to the vessel and assist in recovery operations.*

The master relayed that he was concerned that the vessel could lose power at any time and may sink quickly or capsize. I requested that the master obtain handheld radios should electric power be lost. I passed CG 6031's ETA of twenty minutes to the master. The master constantly was

A photograph taken from CG 1504. *U.S. Coast Guard photograph.*

*asking when the helo would arrive. He mentioned that he would have his
crew muster on the pool deck.*

REEVES. *I can remember just an incredible sense of relief when I heard
that the ship was still afloat.*

Holman directed the *SeaBreeze* skipper to assemble all hands aft on the
uppermost deck, the best location for hoisting. Captain Papadopoulos was
to have the crew form two lines of seventeen each and await the arrival of
the first helicopter.

Captain Papadopoulos had other concerns. He was attempting, with only
one engine and very limited power, to bring the *SeaBreeze* around, heading into
the wind. With what power was available, he applied the left rudder, causing
the massive amount of water in the ship's bowels to shift dramatically, which,
in turn, caused the *SeaBreeze* to roll forty degrees and take on a starboard list
of twenty degrees. It would occasionally list farther to starboard, responding
to the building waves.

1307

The SAR mission coordinator of the Fifth Coast Guard District Rescue
Coordination Center briefed the Air Force Rescue Coordination Center and
the New York Air National Guard concerning the possible use of an Air
Force H-60 for the mission. No actual requests for assistance were made at
that time.

Even with a tail wind, the helicopter had a slower airspeed than the
C-130. This meant that they would have a longer ride in the horrific weather.
Molthen, the seasoned aircraft commander with scores of rescues under his
belt, would later admit that he experienced spatial disorientation. Without a
visible horizon and in the extreme air turbulence, he was uncertain if they
were flying level. With Neubecker backing him up on the flight instruments,
he was reassured that they were.

1313

The navigator aboard Rescue 1504 acquired another surface radar contact
fifteen nautical miles from the *SeaBreeze*, and the C-130 departed the area to

investigate. Holman informed the master of the *SeaBreeze* of their temporary departure and promised to return. Five minutes later, Rescue 1504 arrived at the target and passed over the vessel at two hundred feet. They communicated on channel 16. The vessel was identified as M/V *Patricia*, a 738-foot-long bulk carrier. M/V *Patricia* was also diverted and made the best possible speed in heavy seas.

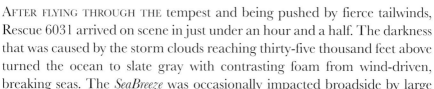

AFTER FLYING THROUGH THE tempest and being pushed by fierce tailwinds, Rescue 6031 arrived on scene in just under an hour and a half. The darkness that was caused by the storm clouds reaching thirty-five thousand feet above turned the ocean to slate gray with contrasting foam from wind-driven, breaking seas. The *SeaBreeze* was occasionally impacted broadside by large waves, sending seawater up to the partially deployed lifeboats. The *SeaBreeze* was in extremis.

Both Molthen and Neubecker saw what was self-evident; the stark realization that *SeaBreeze* could roll over and capsize at any moment added to the urgency of getting the crew off of the vessel, but it also complicated their initial plan. The situation was so dire that they discussed the tremendous risk of lowering Reeves into certain danger. If Reeves was aboard and the *SeaBreeze* capsized, there was little they could do to save one of their own. After assessing the risk and the urgent need to get the *SeaBreeze* crew to safety, they decided to proceed.

1328

The second C-130, which was slated but not launched for the Wright Memorial event, was airborne and left Coast Guard Station Elizabeth City to support the mission. Its call sign was "Rescue 1500."

1329

Molthen brought the helicopter into a hover over the stern of the listing ship. Both pilots saw the *SeaBreeze* crew assembled and waiting for rescue.

The 6031 crew completed the rescue checklist and hoist briefing, including turning the "contingency power" switch on, which would allow the engines to produce maximum power during the hoisting evolutions.

Neubecker saw that there was a steel light cable stretching from the ship's mast to the stern that was encroaching on the hoist area. He called LT Storch in 1504 to contact the *SeaBreeze* captain and get it down while 6031 completed its rescue checklist and hoist briefing. CDR Holman relayed to the captain on the bridge that the cable had to come down to commence the hoisting operations.

Several minutes passed without a response to the helicopter. They agonized that they were burning precious fuel just waiting to have the cable downed. Nothing was happening.

Molthen and Neubecker discussed the urgency of beginning hoist operations, even with the cable in place. They were unsure that the cable could be removed, and in the absence of a response and feeling an increased urgency to get people off the sinking ship, they moved the helicopter closer to the stern and prepared for hoisting, getting dangerously close to the steel cable.

Unbeknownst to the helicopter crew, the captain of the *SeaBreeze* ordered the crew to sever the cable. Then, in close proximity to the *SeaBreeze*, both Neubecker and Molthen suddenly saw the cable whip by them, just missing the rotor. Both instantly realized that the cable could have brought a sudden and fatal end to their rescue efforts, crashing the helicopter into the ship or, even worse, into the water below. Molthen shouted into the aircraft ICS.

MOLTHEN. *Crap!*

Nothing more needed to be said.

HOLMAN. *I believe the ship's safety officer used an axe to cut the electric light cable, probably from an area on the ship's upper decks since the cable, when released, posed a flight safety risk (possible rotor system entanglement) to CG 6031.*

MOLTHEN. *Yeah, the cable was a real problem. It was a few minutes before they cut it down, and when they did, it went sailing by us really close, and I was really concerned. If that cable got into the rotor, we would have gone down.*

Once the cable was down, Molthen brought the helicopter directly over the hoist area. Reeves moved to the open door to view the rolling ship fifty feet below. He had the basket trail line bundled in a pocket for future use. Molthen and Neubecker could no longer see the hoist area.

> MOLTHEN. *Once we are over the hoist area, the pilot and copilot cannot see what is going on below. We are all constantly talking on the ICS. Our flight mechanic and hoist operator, Lorne Green, would constantly give us positioning directions, and it was up to us to interpret the directions into positioning the aircraft. I was mainly focused on Lorne's conning commands. Craig would monitor altitude, drift, engine parameters and everything that I was unable to monitor or see due to my full attention to hoisting and not crashing into the ship.*
>
> *I did get a point of reference early on. I could clearly see the coffee cups on the dining room tables on the cruise ship. I would try to keep them in view as we were continually battling the crosswind, burbles from the disturbed wind coming around the superstructure and smokestacks and, of course, the ship moving up and down in the huge swells. At one point, we were actually looking up at the ship's lifeboats. It was a constant challenge to maintain position for hoisting operations, especially with the AFCS problems we encountered later.*

Green talked to both pilots on the ICS.

> GREEN. *Rescue checklist complete. Ready for deployment of rescue swimmer.*

> MOLTHEN. *Roger, check swimmer.*

> GREEN. *Swimmer ready.*

Green gave Reeves three firm pats on the back to signal that they were ready for him to deploy.

> MOLTHEN. *Begin hoist and conn me in.*

> GREEN. *Swimmer at the door….Swimmer going down.*

Green controled the descent.

REEVES. *At the door, all fear disappears. You focus. Everything has your attention. There is no time for fear.*

Green lowered Reeves, who was clutching the three-sixteenths-of-an-inch steel hoist cable on the way down. Just prior to reaching the angled deck, a strong wind gust hit the helicopter, and Molthen corrected for it. At the same time, a large wave impacted the *SeaBreeze* broadside, raising it up more than twenty feet. The combination of the two events caused Reeves to miss the ship entirely.

REEVES. *I remember looking at the side of the ship, its dark hull about ten feet in front of me. The lifeboats were way above me.*

With Reeves's feet only a few feet above the water, Green brought him up for another try. He told Molthen over the ICS to move to the right. This time, Reeves hit the deck, literally, falling backward on impact due to the steep angle of the rain-soaked deck.

REEVES. *I was deployed to the ship via my harness, and I carried a trail line with me. Once I was on deck, I connected the line to the hoist hook, and they retrieved the hook. They then connected the basket and lowered it back down. I was focused on the hoist operations, so I didn't realize the crowd had gathered around me, and as soon as the basket touched the deck, there were twenty men scrambling to get into it. It was at this point I realized they were all in panic mode. They were diving into the basket and pulling each other out and fighting one another for position.*

Then a crewman brandishing a large hunting knife approached the basket and claimed rights to being hoisted first. Reeves called Molthen on the radio.

REEVES. *Sir, it's a total mob. They're fightin' like pirates here to get into the basket.*

MOLTHEN. *Do you want me to bring you up?*

Commander Holman, monitoring the "on-scene" radio frequency, overheard the predicament unfolding on the *SeaBreeze* fantail. Neubecker radioed the C-130 for help. CDR Holman reached Captain

Papadopoulos on the *SeaBreeze* bridge by radio. The conversation was short and directive.

> HOLMAN. *Take control of your crew! Don't make me come down there to talk to you sir.*

CDR Holman obviously could not leave the airborne C-130 to visit the *SeaBreeze* captain, but in the fray of the "pirate fight," the captain did not know this.

> HOLMAN. *I contacted the master on three separate occasions and directed him to calm his crew and establish order and discipline on the decks to prevent complicating matters and elevating the risk of an already hazardous rescue operation. The Coast Guard rescue swimmer on deck radioed Rescue 6031 and us, [saying] that panic had broken out on deck and that fighting with knives was now going on. I assured the master that all people would be taken off the vessel—"one by one, we leave no one behind." The master left the bridge for the fantail to restore order; the vessel safety officer remained on the bridge to mind the helm.*

There was a feeling of extreme urgency by everyone aboard *SeaBreeze*, including Reeves; they felt the ship was in imminent peril. Listing precariously to starboard and taking a heavy beam sea to port, one large wave might have proven disastrous to the entire rescue operation.

> REEVES. *I could see the fear in their eyes. They knew their own ship, and they were very scared. I thought maybe I should be scared, too.*

The hoisting was further complicated by the rolling and heaving decks. The *SeaBreeze* rose and fell between twenty and thirty feet during the rescue, and on one occasion, it rose to within ten feet of the helicopter. The slope of the deck increased with the crest of each large wave, only to lessen when the ship settled in the next trough. Coupled with a driving rain and relentless wind, balance was precarious.

The basket was subjected to hurricane-force winds that were blowing at over eighty-eight miles per hour. They were blowing the occupied basket as it was being hoisted up and the unoccupied basket as it was being lowered behind the helicopter and temporarily out of view.

Everyone involved then realized the extreme urgency of the situation and the necessity of getting all of the people off of the ship as fast as humanly possible. No one knew how long the ship could stay afloat. Reeves had a novel idea. He would place two adults in the basket per hoist, something that had never been done before.

> REEVES. *I thought we could hoist two at a time. The hoist can lift six hundred pounds, and two people don't weigh that much.*

He chose two of the *SeaBreeze* crewmen to get into the basket. Each crewman had a small carry-on bag, and all were wearing bulky lifejackets with two words stamped on the back: SEABREEZE PANAMA.

The first hoist went well.

> REEVES. *The second time the basket came down, they rushed it again, but I disconnected the basket and, holding the hook and cable, took several steps away from it. I told all of them to line up along the railing by the pool and we would continue two at a time in the order they were lined up, or we will all stay here. Everyone formed a line, except one man remained in the basket and refused to get out. I told him we are not doing anything until he steps into the line with his friends. He argued and refused to get out. I folded my arms and told him we are not going anywhere until he gets in the line with his friends. When he saw that I was serious, he reluctantly got out of the basket and into the line.*

Reeves then went to the knife-bearing crewman in an attempt to disarm him. He demanded the knife. Realizing that Reeves had total control of the operation, the crewman reluctantly handed the knife to Reeves, who immediately threw it into the swimming pool next to the hoist area. The knife man was sent to the back of the line.

Reeves reconnected the hoist hook and trail line to the basket and placed two more crewmen inside. He signaled to Green to hoist. As the basket ascended, Reeves pulled hard on the trail line to reduce the swinging and keep the hoist as vertical as possible.

> REEVES. *Part of the problem was that I could use my body weight to control the basket, and then, the deck would drop out from under me maybe twenty feet. Several times, I was on my back, spinning around on the deck, holding the trail line as hard as I could.*

During the third hoist, a large, cresting wave impacted the side of the *SeaBreeze* and exploded upward, engulfing the entire helicopter. Molthen and Neubecker momentarily lost all visibility through the windshield. Suddenly, the helicopter controls changed. The wave spike swamped the automatic flight control system, totally disabling it. Molthen shouted to Neubecker "AFCS!"

> MOLTHEN. *The AFCS provides computer assist to improve aircraft stability that makes it easier to fly. Loss of the AFCS requires much more concentrated effort by the pilot to fly or maintain hover. We practice the loss of the AFCS, so when it happened, yes, we were very concerned, but Craig got it going again, and that was a real relief. It would go down again several more times, but always come back up for Craig.*

Huge waves continued to batter the *SeaBreeze* broadside and spike upward, dousing the helicopter with saltwater another six times, crashing the AFCS and causing Molthen to grip the controls so tightly that his right hand began to go numb. Each time, Neubecker had to reboot the AFCS. Each time, it returned to life.

They conducted two more hoists, and again, impatient crewmen decided to rush an ascending basket. One grabbed onto the side of the basket, which was already full with two people, and attempted to go up with it, just hanging on the outside. Reeves used hand signals to stop the hoist and peeled off the errant crewman.

A wave spike driving up *SeaBreeze*'s port quarter. *U.S. Coast Guard photograph.*

One crewman brought two large suitcases to the hoist area. Reeves, mostly through sign language, told him that only a small parcel could go and that he should get what was essential from the luggage and leave the rest. He was moved aside and bypassed.

As the basket came down again, a large swell hit the *SeaBreeze*, and the empty basket swung sideways, landing close to the bypassed crewman. The crewman grabbed the basket as if to claim possession. Reeves came over to get the basket for another hoist, and for a moment, he had a tug-of-war with the bypassed crewman. Reeves reclaimed his basket and signaled for two more people, leaving the bypassed person behind, again.

Neubecker called Green on the ICS.

NEUBECKER. *What's our count?*

AMT2 Green was concentrating on stacking up new arrivals to maximize cabin space, and he replied that he was unsure of the count.

Neubecker also saw that the cabin was getting crowded and instructed the new passengers to move toward the cockpit to make more room. Nothing happened. He realized that few, if any, of these people were English-speaking. So, he went to plan B, reaching around the back of his seat and grabbing people, pulling them forward to the cockpit to make more room. If the ship was to go down soon, space and time were of the essence. While this provided more critical space for incoming rescuees, it blocked the view of the cabin from the cockpit, making it impossible to maintain an accurate head count.

NEUBECKER. *We all agreed that we were going to keep hoisting until 6001 was on scene so we could save as many as possible before the ship sank.*

REEVES. *Every time I looked up at Lorne, he was giving me a hand signal for two more. So, I sent two more.*

Twenty minutes after arriving at the ship, Rescue 6031 was approaching "bingo fuel."

HOLMAN. *"Bingo fuel" is a predetermined fuel state that takes into account the distance to return to a landing site considering aircraft performance, weight and weather conditions, plus some extra reserve fuel for "mom and the kids" should an in-flight emergency have to be dealt with.*

Neubecker called the C-130 that was circling above and reported that they were fifty pounds from bingo fuel. At the same time, Green reported to Molthen that they had a full house and that there was no more room for people. Molthen called for the return of his rescue swimmer, but Reeves demurred. He wanted to stay on the *SeaBreeze* and support the next helicopter. Molthen didn't like the idea at all and directed Reeves to leave the basket and trail line on the *SeaBreeze* for the second helicopter and return.

> MOLTHEN. *We did not have good information as to when Randy (Rescue 6001) would arrive. Rescue 1504 was handling comms for us, and we did not have direct comms with the second helicopter. Darren [Reeves] was part of my crew, and I wanted him back aboard. I thought the ship would roll over any minute. I was worried for Darren's safety.*

Molthen told Green to bring Reeves aboard. Green looked down at Reeves and gave him the "cutthroat" hand signal.

> REEVES. *After an eternity of hoists, I got the signal from the hoist operator. I assured the remaining men the second aircraft would recover them. I disconnected the basket and left it and the trail line on the deck and was recovered via my harness.*

The rescue swimmer AST1 Darren Reeves was hoisted up to the door of the helicopter.

> REEVES. *When I got to the door, I got a little surprise. There was no room. People were actually slightly bulging out of the doorway. I grabbed the two handrails on each side of the door to force myself into the cabin enough to possibly clear the door. Lorne was not able to close the door with his hands but managed to push the door closed with his foot. I heard sounds of people in pain.*

1359

The second helicopter, Rescue 6001, was on the scene. LCDR Watson and ENS Bonn positioned themselves about one thousand yards astern of the *SeaBreeze*, waiting for the first helicopter to retrieve their rescue swimmer.

Rescue 6031 banks left into the wind with a full load. Rescue swimmer Reeves can be seen below the helicopter. *Steve Bonn photograph.*

1405

Rescue 6031 yawed and banked left into the wind, leaving the *SeaBreeze*. Molthen realized the helicopter had probably then exceeded its maximum gross weight of 21,884 pounds.

> MOLTHEN. *I figured we were a little bit over that, but, you know, you gotta do what you gotta do.*

Molthen and Neubecker slid off the port side of the ship in an attempt to transition to forward flight. Both were very aware that leaving a hover and transitioning to forward flight would result in a loss of altitude. Being only fifty feet above the wave tops with an overloaded helicopter already hovering at maximum power left no room for error. They were counting on the eighty-seven-mile-per-hour crosswind to help them.

> NEUBECKER. *If not simultaneously compensated for by adding forward cyclic and more collective pitch, helicopters will normally dip down in altitude while going through effective translational lift or ETL. Of course, when you are already at maximum power with the collective like we were,*

we couldn't increase the collective anymore, so we knew we would just have to accept the drop in altitude until we were through ETL. We just hoped that the drop in altitude would not bring us down to the height of the waves.

Then came the moment of truth. Molthen saw the helicopter was actually moving down toward the water. He was losing altitude. He told Neubecker that they would need to get more airspeed. Using all the available power that the helicopter could provide, the rotor blades bit into the air for all their worth as the helicopter dipped, then leveled off low and, finally, slowly started to rise, leaving the ship behind.

MOLTHEN. *With that crosswind, I was probably already in translational lift. That's when the main rotor blade gets enough wind over the blade and acts like a big wing. We wanted to get more air speed, heading into the wind to get more lift. That's what we did. We did settle toward the water a bit until we gained more airspeed, not a very comfortable feeling.*

Rescue 6001 quickly moved into hoisting position.

Reeves knew that his ICS connection was on the other side of the helicopter cabin. After some thought, he decided to squeeze through the eighteen inches of space between the cabin overhead (ceiling) and the glob of humans below. He pulled his way across the cabin to connect his headset, never touching the cabin floor.

As Rescue 6031 departed from the area, Neubecker made a radio transmission to Rescue 1504, the on-scene commander, with advice for the crew of the next rescue helicopter.

NEUBECKER. *1504, just be advised, those guys may have some trouble. Uh, we just talked to our rescue swimmer where people with knives are fightin' on deck to come up. So be aware of that.*

For example, when the swimmer goes down make sure he watches for weapons because they were fighting to get in the basket.

He continued with a report of his head count.

NEUBECKER. *We have a full load here. We can't even count how many we've got. We think we have seventeen count but unable to confirm that. We can't count because people are so mangled in here.*

As soon as the first helicopter cleared the ship, Watson brought Rescue 6001 into a hover over the *SeaBreeze* stern. The rescue swimmer for Rescue 6001, Bob Florisi, saw the basket and trail line left by the first helicopter still on the deck. He approached the door, clipped his harness to the hoisting hook and prepared to be lowered to the wallowing *SeaBreeze* below. Even though there was a basket and trail line already on deck, Florisi, as is standard practice, also deployed with his own bundled trail line. Not known to him at the time, this would later prove to be incredibly important when he encountered the unexpected.

He reached the rolling decks, disconnected the hook from his harness and connected the hoist line to the basket left by the first helicopter. He signaled for only one person to approach, but three people rushed the basket. Florisi waved off two of the approaching crewmen and loaded only one into the basket. All of the hoists conducted by Rescue 6001 would be singles. He signaled Pulliam to raise the basket and grabbed the trail line to control the ascent in the strong crosswinds.

> FLORISI. *One of the biggest problems was footing. I would be controlling the basket with the trail line, and the deck would drop out from under me. It was very difficult to maintain a constant pressure on the trail line.*

On the second hoist, with a combination of wind working on the basket being raised and the ship's deck falling out from under him, Florisi lost his footing and was dragged aft by the strong crosswind, stopping just short of a stairwell down to a lower deck. The basket and its occupant were blown behind the helicopter, making the retrieval by the flight mechanic more challenging. As the basket reached the helicopter, Florisi regained his footing and prepared for the next hoist.

On the third hoist, Florisi hand signaled for AET2 Sam Pulliam to raise the next person. An exceptionally strong wind gust caught the ascending basket, blowing it and its occupant behind the helicopter.

> FLORISI. *At that point, I was being dragged across the wet deck and toward a stairwell servicing a lower level. It was no longer a matter of footing; I was running out of deck.*

Florisi used his entire body weight and strength to hold his ground, but the unrelenting wind had other ideas. In pulling back against the wind, he made a final stand, leaning back and pulling as hard as possible to control the ascent. Suddenly, the weak link on the trail line broke, sending him down hard on his back, crashing to the deck.[39]

The basket, then without any control from below, was captured by the wind, blew far behind the helicopter, and disappeared from view. With the basket then positioned behind the helicopter, the hoist cable became wedged between the external fuel tank and the fuselage. Pulliam worked to manually pull the cable forward and cleared the fuel tank to resume the hoist. He wrestled the heavy basket aboard with its shaken occupant and noticed that the trail line was missing. Over the ICS, he reported the problem to the pilots.

Florisi quickly got upright, gathered the broken trail line and threw it down into the stairwell.

After getting the *SeaBreeze* crewman moved to the back of the cabin, Pulliam then had to deploy an empty basket in hurricane-force winds without any assistance from below. Once it was out of the helicopter, the basket again caught the crosswind and disappeared from view. Although it took extra time, he attempted to control the descent through a combination of helicopter steering commands and dampening the hoist cable. When the basket swung over the deck near Florisi, Pulliam executed a sudden release of the cable, giving the basket a hard landing but on target.

With the broken trail line removed from the hoist area, Florisi unbundled the trail line that he brought with him. Less than ten seconds were lost in connecting the new line. The fourth hoist was more controlled.

As additional people were being hoisted, LCDR Watson wanted more power.

WATSON. *Contingency power coming on.*

BONN. *There is a toggle switch on the collective that the pilot can flip on with his thumb. This changes the temperature limit settings in the engine to allow it to provide just a little bit more power if we need it for high-demand situations. We don't fly with it turned on all the time. It's only used in emergencies when one engine fails or when we need to temporarily increase the max temperature limit of the engine in operations like this.*

THE PILOTS OF THE first helicopter had a critical decision to make.

> NEUBECKER. *From the weather forecast, weather radar and satellite images we looked at prior to launch, we all knew we were going to be facing severe weather conditions both there and back. But the weather system was moving to the northeast, which meant that the shortest distance to shore would actually keep us in the heavy weather and headwinds longer. So, Dan and I discussed what our primary and alternate destinations would be as we were departing the scene. I recommended that instead of heading for NASA Wallops, which was a little closer, that we should instead head for NAS Oceana.[40] While it was a little further distance-wise, we would probably be able to break out of the weather earlier and therefore have more favorable winds sooner.*
>
> *Having spent some time on that base with my brother Scott, who was in the Navy in Norfolk, I knew we would be able to get the medical, immigration, and law enforcement support we needed at Oceana. We didn't know if we would have any more "pirate" shenanigans like Darren encountered on deck, but if so, we wanted law enforcement there just in case. NAS Oceana also had fuel readily available, so they could provide us with all the fuel we would need to make it home. Dan agreed, so we headed to Oceana with Wallops as our alternate.*

Still providing cover for CG 6001 as they hoisted the remaining *SeaBreeze* crew, LT Storch in Rescue 1504 called CG 6031 on the radio about their intentions. Rescue 1504 needed to know where CG6031 was headed so they could eventually catch up and provide cover for both helicopters back to land.

> STORCH. *31, 04. What's your position in relation to the vessel?*

> NEUBECKER. *We're headed…we're going to try for Oceana. If we can't make Oceana, we're going for NASA Wallops.*

> STORCH. *Say altitude.*

> NEUBECKER. *Three hundred feet.*

After two hours of flying in the "goo," and another twenty minutes hovering over *SeaBreeze*, close enough to see coffee cups on the dining room tables, it was time to switch drivers.

MOLTHEN. *A few minutes after leaving the ship, Craig took over the flying, and I worked comms and the instruments. I was somewhat physically and mentally exhausted.*

About fifteen minutes into the flight, a rescued crewman at the bottom of the heap experienced uncontrolled anxiety, either from claustrophobia or raw fear as the helicopter drove through severe turbulence and incessant lightning. There was a minor movement of the heap of people as the panicked individual attempted to free himself from impinging crew mates. There was nowhere for him to go. Soon, he realized that his efforts at freedom were useless. With consoling words from another crewman, he and the rest of the rescuees accepted their plight and settled in for the duration.

Reeves had another concern. His greatest fear was that someone would vomit. He figured this would cause a chain reaction, and twenty-six people throwing up inside a small helicopter would lead to disaster.

REEVES. *We had severe turbulence on the return as well. I was just praying that no one got airsick, because if one person does, they will all get sick. Although we had no food to offer them, I did have one bottle of water and offered to share it with them, but no one wanted water.*

CAPTAIN PAPADOPOULOS CALLED THE C-130 that was still orbiting above.

PAPADOPOULOS. *Coast Guard, this is* SeaBreeze *bridge.*

HOLMAN. SeaBreeze *bridge, Coast Guard.*

PAPADOPOULOS. *Okay, you have all the rest of the crew. I am the last one on the bridge. Should I leave the bridge?*

HOLMAN. *Yes, sir. Leave the bridge, all people. Chopper's over the stern. Go now.*

The captain left the bridge, and at that moment, the *SeaBreeze* was no longer under command. Captain Solon Papadopoulos was captain in name only. The *SeaBreeze* had another master.

As Captain Papadopoulos reached the hoist area, there were only two people remaining to be hoisted by Rescue 6001. Rescue swimmer Florisi placed the second-to-last person in the basket. The hurricane-force wind again asserted its presence against the ascending basket, sending it far behind the helicopter and swinging. Pulliam gained control and brought the person into the cabin. Either through fear from the hoist or possibly great relief from being saved, the rescued crewman lost control of his bowels and defecated in his clothing.

Florisi saw that there was only one person left in the hoist area. He asked the captain if he was the last one. The answer was yes. Captain Papadopoulos left his ship, never to return.

Papadopoulos was the eighth person to be hoisted by the second helicopter. He reached the cabin door and was pulled into the cabin by Pulliam. All of the seats were already occupied. Pulliam talked to Watson on the ICS.

PULLIAM. *Let me get these guys to stack up some more.*

WATSON. *Okay, they've got to sit on each other's laps.*

Expecting a total of seventeen people to be rescued, Florisi realized that only eight crewmen had been hoisted. The math didn't add up. With Rescue 1504 still circling the scene below the cloud deck, Rescue 6001 made an alarming report that it only had eight people hoisted from *SeaBreeze*, including the captain. It would have been impossible to fit twenty-six rescuees into the first helicopter. Perhaps the initial count was wrong. Maybe there were still others aboard the ship who did not make it to the hoist area. This was a real concern for Commander Holman.

Holman directed Florisi to quickly check the ship's passageways to look for any remaining crewmen. He did and saw no one. He returned to the hoist area, entered the basket and gave a hand signal to be hoisted.

Captain Papadopoulos was not the last person to leave the *SeaBreeze*—that would be AST3 Robert Florisi.

With a full load of people, 6031 encountered the main storm front that was standing between them and the safety of shore. Hurricane-force headwinds reduced their "over the water" speed to less than ninety knots, about half of the helicopter's maximum cruising speed. Neubecker recalled that his wind speed indicator showed that they were bucking a seventy-six-knot headwind. Flying was further complicated by more lightning and unrelenting severe turbulence.

Headwinds and weight greatly increased their fuel consumption, and in an effort to save every last drop of precious fuel, Molthen decided to turn off the cabin air conditioning.

> Molthen. *We turned off the AC to conserve fuel. We also had a secondary landing spot if fuel became a real issue. We had to make a quick decision to fly to Oceana. We would not have been able to change destinations midflight due to fuel.*

With the air conditioning turned off, the cabin temperature quickly rose to over one hundred degrees.

> Reeves. *It was painful. All of us in the flight crew were wearing dry suits. I was swimming in sweat.*

Neubecker asked Reeves if he could open the window vent (on the far side of the cabin). Reeves struggled to get to the window—again crawling over bodies below—and, using the arm of a rescuee as an extension, opened the vent, bringing some relief to the huddled mass.

> Neubecker. *Did you open the vent?*

> Reeves. *Yes, sir—and three people fell out.*

It was the only humor for the entire flight. With the window opened, Reeves remained atop the heap of humanity, spreading his weight as evenly as possible.

Still unsure of the actual count, Molthen passed a notepad back to Reeves and instructed him to have each person sign their name. Over half an hour passed before the notepad was returned to the cockpit. There were only twelve names.

The two-hour flight to safety was a personal challenge to all. Any mechanical mishap could have proven to be disastrous, and although flight crews are trained in egress from a ditched helicopter, there would have been no way for all of them to successfully leave a sinking helicopter that was carrying this many people.

Neubecker would later admit that he silently enlisted the help of God to make the return flight of Rescue 6031 a safe one for all.

EVEN THOUGH BOTH HELICOPTERS had left the *SeaBreeze*, Commander Holman was still concerned about the head count. He was reluctant to leave *SeaBreeze* without further effort. Both helicopters required the C-130 escort to safety, but Holman circled the *SeaBreeze* five more times before leaving. He dropped down to almost wave height to surveil the ship, but there was no sign of life.

The second C-130, Rescue 1500, would soon be on scene to continue the surveillance.

> HOLMAN. *When I talked with the 1500, I asked them to get low and slow. Make noise so that if there is someone inside, they can hear you.*

1415

Rescue 1504 contacted USS *Saipan*, M/V *Front Rider* and M/V *Patricia* by radio to release them from the incident, and with a personal note of gratitude, they thanked them for their support. Commander Holman and his flight crew left the abandoned ship to fly "cover" for the two returning helicopters.

> HOLMAN. *We escorted the CG-6001 to Naval Air Station Oceana, Virginia. I stayed below the weather with them going back. We kept the CG-6001 in-sight always. We "formed-up" on them occasionally. We could see how crammed the helo was, but I mostly flew in-trail* [slightly behind them—"S" turning].
>
> *My job was to provide SAR support for the helo should they have to ditch and provide communications and coordination for 6031's arrival at Oceana. I was also in communication with both the other helos and the other C-130. I also was able to talk to the air defense* [Navy VACAPES

controller] *people to let them know we were coming back into the "air-defense zone" so they would not intercept us.*

Proceeding to scene, SeaBreeze from Elizabeth City, we prepped the C-130 for immediate raft deployment should any helo go in the water. Our drop master placed a deployable raft kit on the aircraft ramp. We were ready to "open-up" the back of the aircraft immediately and deploy rafts. Such a deployment would have been a real challenge in those weather conditions.

In addition to escorting our rescue helicopters, we had to coordinate the survivors' arrival at Naval Air Station Oceana, Virginia, instead of NASA Wallops Island airfield on the Virginia Eastern Shore. U.S. Customs, Immigration and Agriculture were required upon the aircraft landing at Oceana. Security was a concern as well. The Coast Guard Rescue Coordination Center at Portsmouth, Virginia, provided timely assistance in having these agencies present on our arrival; all was accomplished in an outstanding manner considering the short lead time. In retrospect, Navy Oceana was the perfect recovery point for the SeaBreeze survivors.

1418

With eight of the *SeaBreeze* crew in the cabin, Rescue 6001 began the long flight to safety. They switched drivers, and the weather worsened.

BONN. *Randy* [Watson] *did all of the flying for the beginning portion of the rescue. The hoists were obviously very physically demanding due to the high waves and winds and the movement of the ship. We did get splashed with sea spray from the waves hitting the ship but never got "doused." After we completed the hoists and were headed to Oceana, Randy gave me the controls to fly so he could take a break.*

We started at five hundred feet, and at the time, the clouds were high enough above us and the visibility was at least three miles but hazy with mist and some rain. As we made our way to the coast, the weather continued to deteriorate. The C-130 let us know that there was a line of thunderstorms in our way since they were able to scan the weather a little better with their radar and could get a better look at it. Our normal plan would be to try to circumnavigate any dangerous storm cells like this, but in this case, it extended too far north and south for us to be able to get around it with the amount of fuel we had. So, we had no choice but to just barrel through it.

As we continued, the cloud layer kept getting lower, and the winds picked up, creating more turbulence. I kept descending to stay out of the clouds so that we could still see the water, but this soon became a little too dangerous. We were now at three hundred feet, but the turbulence was getting bad enough that it was causing us to climb or descend more than one hundred feet at a time very rapidly. If I tried to get any lower to stay out of the clouds, we were worried that the turbulence could just push us down into the ocean.

We decided that our best option would be to climb up to one thousand feet into the clouds and continue on instruments so we were not so close to the water. I transferred my focus now completely on the instruments and climbed into the clouds. I leveled off at one thousand feet and the turbulence continued to increase in intensity along with the rain becoming very heavy, and now, we were beginning to see flashes of lightning.

In the aviation world, we are always taught this is the last place you would ever want to be in an aircraft.

In the clouds, on instruments, we normally let the autopilot maintain our altitude to make everything easy. The turbulence was so bad, however, that the autopilot was not able to hold our altitude safely because it required such extreme power adjustments. Randy turned off the autopilot for me, and I just flew it by hand. I also gave up trying to stay at one altitude because I had to make so many extreme power adjustments. I finally just concentrated on keeping the helicopter level and let our altitude go where it may, as long as we didn't start descending too close toward the ocean.

The sound of the heavy rain hitting the aircraft was loud enough to actually get in the way of hearing the radios. The lightning became so frequent it looked like we were surrounded by strobe lights and I was actually starting to cringe because I was so sure we were going to get struck by lightning. I don't know how, but luckily, we never did.

Even though it was the middle of the day, the clouds were so thick in the middle of the thunderstorm that it felt like we were sitting under a wool blanket in the daylight. It was to the point that we turned on our interior lights, aptly named "thunderstorm lights," so I could see the instruments. The turbulence continued to toss us up and down for several minutes, and the only thing I was really controlling was keeping the helicopter level and pointed in the right direction.

At one point, we hit a wind shear line that made us decelerate so rapidly it felt exactly like stopping at the end of a roller coaster ride, pressing our bodies against the shoulder straps holding us in our seats. I can only imagine what all the people in the back were going through without seatbelts.

1425

Rescue 1500 arrived to see the dying ship still afloat. They passed over the ship close enough to vibrate its hull plates. After several passes and seeing no one else emerge, they dropped a data marker buoy and headed back to Air Station Elizabeth City. On the return, they joined up with the third helicopter, Rescue 6026, which was also battling severe weather, and provided an escort for them back to Coast Guard Air Station Elizabeth City.

〰••〰

AN HOUR AND A half into the return flight, Neubecker and Molthen in Rescue 6031 reviewed the distance to shore and the remaining fuel. It looked good—good enough to turn the air conditioner back on. This brought a welcome relief to the rescuees and crew.

An hour from the beach, Rescue 6031 broke out into clear weather. The severe weather front was behind them.

NEUBECKER. *Yeah, we had great visibility then, but we also had incredibly strong headwinds. It was reassuring, however, because when we broke out of the clouds, we could see the shoreline at a distance. I thought to myself that I have never been so happy to see Virginia Beach.*

In the back of the cabin, Reeves could only look down.

REEVES. *When I saw the beach below, I knew that we were close. What a great sight.*

Rescue 1504 providing an escort to NAS Oceana after breaking out into clear weather. *Steve Bonn photograph.*

1630

Rescue 6031 arrived at Naval Air Station Oceana.

MOLTHEN. *We decided to do a hover taxi to the landing area that they assigned us. We were concerned that we might get some sort of reaction from the rescuees the moment we landed, so we wanted to be stopped if we were going to have any issues.*

Molthen talked to Reeves on the ICS and wanted him to count heads by physically touching each person as they emerged from the helicopter. Some rescuees had trouble walking from the two hours of immobility and cramped confinement; others bent over and kissed the tarmac. Due to the language barrier, not much was said to the aircrew, but by gestures and handshakes, they knew that the rescuees were thankful.

AST1 Reeves would later report that one of the rescued crewmen took his hand, not for a handshake, but to hold for a momentary squeeze. His eyes spoke volumes, but no words were exchanged.

Reeves counted a total of twenty-six people. He walked over to Molthen to give the report. Knowing that jamming twenty-six people into a helicopter that was designed to carry a maximum of ten was next to impossible, but not wanting to show any sign of amazement, he replied to Reeves.

Molthen. *Okay. That's a good day's work.*

Almost ten minutes later, Rescue 6001 also landed at NAS Oceana and released its passengers. Rescue 1504 soon followed. The total flight time for each aircraft exceeded four and a half hours.

As soon as the second helicopter was shut down, Molthen walked over and talked to the aircrew of 6001.

Molthen. *I went over to the helicopter and talked to Randy. When the captain got out of Randy's helicopter, we shook hands. There was little said. He was very thankful.*

Molthen and Papadopoulos never met again.

The local media was anxious to interview Captain Papadopoulos. During each interview, he repeated the dire circumstances that were facing him and his crew and his deepest appreciation to the Coast Guard flight crews for "literally saving [their] lives."

With the flight crew interviews with the local media completed, they gassed up the two helicopters and the C-130 for the final flight back to Elizabeth City. There was little discussion on the short flight home. Everyone was tired and hungry. Having had no food on the aircraft, they looked forward to the waiting box lunches they had left behind in the cooler earlier that day.

Lieutenant Molthen gets a pat on the arm from Captain Papadopoulos. *U.S. Coast Guard photograph, PAC Eric Eggen.*

1830

Both 6031 and 6001 arrived at Coast Guard Air Station Elizabeth City. They found that the food they had left behind earlier that morning was gone. They speculated that "the C-130 guys," known for their well-established reputation of being "box lunch hoarders," did the deed. The C-130 guys, of course, denied culpability, but regardless, the food was gone.

They "buttoned up" the aircraft, did some preliminary paperwork, and the helicopter air crews headed home for a hot shower and a late dinner. Some were too tired to eat.

The crew of the CG 1504 was not so lucky. After arriving at Air Station Elizabeth City, they remained on board to resume their search and rescue watch standing duties, since they had not exceeded their flight hour limitations.

> HOLMAN. *I called my wife to tell her about my day. I told her how lucky we all were today—she could not believe we flew in that weather.*
>
> *My earlier prayer when we lifted off from Elizabeth City at 1200 noon was heard by God.*

> MOLTHEN. *By the time I got home, the kids were already asleep. I'm not sure that I ate anything. Probably had a glass of single malt scotch and slept upstairs so as to not awaken the kids.*

> REEVES. *I got home at 1100 that night. I don't remember eating anything. I just needed sleep.*

> NEUBECKER. *I didn't make it home until much later in the evening after the mission. The media requests had already started to pour in about the rescue, and I was the Air Station's Public Affairs Officer. I fielded the calls and began coordinating with LCDR McPherson and his staff at LANTAREA/D5 Public Affairs in Portsmouth, Virginia. When I finally did make it home, I laid in bed and prayed and thanked God for keeping us safe and for allowing us to make a successful rescue. I tried to fall asleep, but between the adrenaline from the rescue and all the media calls, I didn't get much sleep that night. It turned out to only be a precursor of what the next day would hold.*

It was a long day with a lot of adrenaline for the Coast Guard pilots and aircrews, but they went home to their families and brought a grateful cargo ashore with them. Coast Guard 6031 did not participate in the flyover of the Wright Brothers Memorial earlier that day, but the fixed-wing aircraft and helicopters that participated in the *SeaBreeze* rescue were a true testimonial to recognize the ninety-seventh anniversary of powered flight. And, perhaps, even Igor Sikorsky was smiling down from above.

Little did the crew know that their duty was not yet finished. The next day, the onslaught of media would begin.

THE MORNING AFTER

hat Monday was a day of contrasts. There was jubilation and relief from the crew of the *SeaBreeze* and their families. The *SeaBreeze* crewmen were given food and lodging, and many called internationally to families at home to say that they were safe and well. Some of the crew who remained in the area around Naval Air Station Oceana were interviewed by the media. All of those who were interviewed openly expressed—sometimes emotionally—their sincere gratitude to those in the Coast Guard who went into harm's way to save them. They universally spoke of wanting to be reunited with family.

But there were other "doings" that day as well.

REEVES. *It was 0500 in the morning when my phone rang at home. When I went to bed late the night before, I was exhausted and looked forward to sleeping in. It was not a duty day for me; the weekend duty meant that I had the next day off. I was awakened from a deep sleep by the phone and heard a person identifying himself as a radio newscaster at a local radio station. Somehow, he got my home phone number and wanted the story of the rescue. I really can't recall much of that conversation, and at that time in the morning, I must have sounded pretty funny.*

After I hung up the phone and tried to get back to sleep, the phone rang again. I was going to let it ring, thinking it was just another news person. However, I decided to answer it. It was the Air Station calling and telling me to get in as soon as possible.

NEUBECKER. *I was at work around 0430 the next morning. I was a little groggy from the lack of sleep, but now knowing it was going to be a very busy day with national news media outlets sending satellite trucks to the Air Station for interviews. LCDR McPherson and his staff at LANTAREA/ D5 Public Affairs were handling print media requests from the likes of the Associated Press, the* New York Times, *the* Wall Street Journal, *the* Washington Post *and the* Los Angeles Times, *in addition to seemingly every aviation trade publication in the United States, not to mention lining up the TV media.*

Needless to say, their small staff was kept very, very busy, so they could only spare one public affairs specialist to come down to Elizabeth City to assist us. The satellite trucks began arriving early in the morning, so I was there to meet them and show them where they could setup for the interviews they wanted to conduct. Coast Guard crews, by their very nature, shun the limelight, however, so getting crews to stand in front of the cameras on live national television was a bit of a challenge. The day before, at NAS Oceana, both Dan and Randy had already declined to be interviewed and said with a grin that "the interviews were the Public Affairs Officer's job—so you do it."

The first two satellite trucks to arrive that morning were from ABC and CBS. They wanted live interviews for ABC's Good Morning America *and CBS's* Morning Show. *So, to make that happen at roughly the same time, we set up the TV crews in opposite corners of the hangar with the helicopter in the background and had them ready to go. Darren and I first did the live* Good Morning America *interview, and then we quickly headed over to the opposite corner of the hanger to do the live* Morning Show *interview, where the CBS crew was set up.*

LCDR Brendan Mcpherson, with the Atlantic Area Public Affairs Office in Portsmouth, Virginia, coordinated the print media. The story of the *SeaBreeze* rescue was the lead story on the front page of the *Washington Post*. Other papers and periodicals sought access to the flight crews, and Brendan did his best to accommodate their requests. It would take weeks for the media interest to wane, but the first day after the rescue, the press wanted to see the faces of those who flew into danger to save others in peril. Eventually, all eight helicopter crew members would appear together on national television.

〜・〜

Along with jubilation and recognition, there was also disbelief. Air Station Executive Officer Commander Rod Ansley received a telephone call from Coast Guard Headquarters in Washington, D.C. They had reviewed the situation report (SITREP) of the rescue the day before. They informed him that it was incorrect and asked for correct information as to the number rescued by CG 6031.

> ANSLEY. *They told me outright that one helicopter could not hold twenty-six people in addition to the crew. I told them that the SITREP was correct, and that the helicopter rescued twenty-six people. It was a short conversation.*

It was also a day of uncertainty. When Rescue 1500 left the scene the afternoon before, the *SeaBreeze* was still afloat—foundering, owned by the sea—but still afloat. It was necessary to locate its exact position and advise shipping along the Eastern Seaboard of a "hazard to navigation." The *SeaBreeze* was twenty-one thousand tons of ship at sea with no captain or crew.

0900

Coast Guard Atlantic Area directed the launch of another C-130 mission. The aircraft was CG 1504 with a different aircrew. The directive stated

NARRATIVE CG1504 TASKED TO LOCATE M/V SEA BREEZE 1 TO DETERMINE IF AFLOAT AND POSING A HAZARD TO NAVIGATION.

Among the many requests from the media, several expressed an interest in videotaping the foundering ship. Realizing that they could not accommodate all of the requests, LCDR Brendan McPherson chose two civilians from a local television station to join the flight in search of *SeaBreeze* and make their video available to others. They would be disappointed.

1046

CG 1504 departed Coast Guard Air Station Elizabeth City and headed east to the ship's last-known position. With weather abating and improved visibility, it should have been easy to find it. The aircrew also applied "set and drift" estimates to further refine their target area.

1200

CG 1504 arrived at the most probable location for the *SeaBreeze*, according to the calculations of the aircrew, and commenced a search. Visibility was excellent, but there was no ship.

1206

CG 1504 spotted a debris field and dropped down to the water for a closer look. The SITREP narrative read:

A/C ARRIVED ON SCENE TO FIND A 5 NM BY 2 NM DEBRIS FIELD STRECHING EAST TO WEST. FIELD CONTAINED APPROX 10 LIFERAFTS AND THREE LIFEBOATS

A photograph taken from CG 1504. *U.S. Coast Guard photograph.*

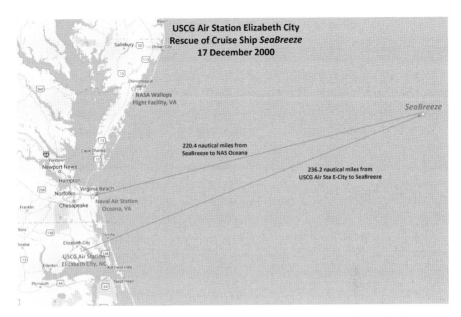

The flight path of an aircraft from Coast Guard Air Station Elizabeth City to *SeaBreeze* and returning to NAS Oceana. *Graphic courtesy of Craig Neubecker.*

(1 OVERTURNED), AS WELL AS DECK CHAIRS, LIFE RINGS, AND OTHER FLOTSAM INDICATIVE OF A CRUISE SHIP. NO OIL SHEEN SEEN. CG1504 MADE 5 PASSES OVER FIELD THEN RTB.

The events of the day took an unexpected turn. In the afternoon, both helicopter aircraft commanders were summoned to the commanding officer's office.

ODOM. *I received a call from the District Office. They wanted to set up a conference call with me and both helicopter pilots. I asked Dan and Randy to come to my office.*

MOLTHEN. *Randy and I were asked to go to see the CO. When we got there, there was a conference call with the senior staff of the Fifth Coast Guard District. We had no idea why a meeting was called and why so many senior officers at district were on the call.*

They asked several questions about not getting the headcount right and if we really needed to overload the helicopter. We told them that we felt that the ship could go over on its side at any time, and we wanted to get as many people off in the shortest time possible.[41]

I told them that at no time did I feel that it was unsafe. We had all the power and all the lift we needed.

ODOM. *I began to feel that the questions to the pilots were becoming somewhat accusatory. I interjected and told them, "I would have done the same thing." I also told the District staff that any further questions should be directed to me. That was, as I recall, pretty much the end of the conference call.*

Molthen recalled pointed questions from some in attendance who were trying to "second guess" their judgment and, by implication, suggest that he was worthy of reprimand, not award. They were also very aware that Molthen was a veteran of many heroic rescues and had already been awarded the Distinguished Flying Cross. When Molthen said they were working in exigent circumstances, he was to be believed. It was his opinion that the ship would have soon sunk, and it did.

Around 1700, Captain Odom's phone rang. It was Vice Admiral Shkor from Coast Guard Atlantic Area. He called to reassure Odom, stating that they were just getting information and not trying to second-guess anyone. He offered his congratulations.

Although the Air Station would soon return to normal routine operations, the flight crew of CG 6031 was just beginning months of recognition and award.

13

ORDINARY PEOPLE DOING EXTRAORDINARY THINGS

Unfortunately, we are a label society. Descriptors such as *boring, over-achiever, passive-aggressive* and hundreds of others tend to distort and oversimplify the complexity of human thought, emotion and behavior. Many, if not most, of these labels are subjective in nature and do not really help one understand people but rather judge them. Some labels, however, offer true insight to a person's character; *hero* is one of them.

In a recent interview, Chesley "Sully" Sullenberger, the pilot of the famed U.S. Airways Flight 1549 that ditched in the Hudson River, was asked about why he was uncomfortable being called a "hero."

Very early on, I had to make an intellectual compromise with myself to graciously accept people's gifts of their gratitude and their putting a label on it. What I thought and what my wife, Lorrie, thought, was that this situation was thrust upon us. We didn't choose to rush into a burning building and rescue someone to put ourselves at risk. But I know that people appreciate heroic acts, and I think that there are a lot of people that day who rose to that level—passengers, crew, rescuers, first responders—and I just think it's natural to celebrate that.

I think the other reason that I initially resisted that label is I think that so many times in our culture that we overuse that word. And by overusing it, I think, we diminish it. And we shouldn't cheapen it, because when it's used appropriately, it's a word that describes the best of what it means to be human.

For the most part, those who serve in the military are also reluctant to use that word. Interestingly, it is not part of military doctrine but an acquired trait that becomes part of a more pervasive military culture.

In a free-association society, we tend to gather, associate and socialize with like-minded people. This is true in a spectrum of activities from religion to politics. For those who have made the military a career, the culture of honor, respect and devotion to duty is commonly shared and practiced. Character and behavior in and among the military community is somewhat predictable, and often, it is very different from what one might expect from civilians.

Most Americans have never been on a military base to witness the unspoken but pervasive culture among those who have chosen to serve. A military base is quite different from the rest of America. Trash is never seen along the roadways. On-base housing is kept clean and quiet, as if there was "pride of ownership" in base housing. There is no need to lock your car on base (although some probably do), and when you see a sailor walking alone, you stop and offer a ride. Neighborhoods quickly coalesce around a family experiencing tragedy, even if they have never met before. Military families can move from base to base every three years and expect to meet the same experience among their new neighbors—and they are rarely disappointed.

Necessarily, boot camp and the ensuing years of military life are responsible for much of this "like-mindedness." Some of this culture becomes so ingrained that it sticks with you. Interestingly, the use of the honorific "sir" or "ma'am" is often carried off base and after service.

So, what is it that makes military people so reticent to use the word *hero* to personally acknowledge their own acts of heroism?

The public witnesses the Coast Guard performing heroic acts routinely, but it is part of the Coast Guard ethos that drives them to shun the label. Trying to describe the Coast Guard ethos is amazingly difficult. Put "Coast Guard ethos" into your search engine and you will find a Coast Guard website to tell you what it is. But much like mission statements, strategic objectives, mottos and creeds, it does not tell the full story.

English is a fascinating language. We have over twenty terms to describe various colors of horses. Species of common animals have different terms according to gender and age—goose, gander and gosling. But oddly, there is no single word that fully describes the deliberately muted reaction of a Coast Guard officer or enlisted person who has just saved someone's life. In the absence of a single word, perhaps it is best to describe what happens among the crew when the rescue mission is over; paperwork is done, and it is time to drive home after a twelve-hour day. The crew member may be greeted with reheated lasagna because the kids have already gone to bed. Little is said about the horrific conditions they just encountered to save another. The report card will mention saving a life or lives, but it will always be in the context of "the crew" or "we" but never "I." When the mission is not "successful," meaning the crew didn't get there in time to save a life, there is little discussion at home, and the spouses don't pry.

The same reaction is true for the military awards given to people who have done truly heroic things. Depending on the occasion, the station or base personnel are assembled, and the commanding officer, officer in charge or some other higher-ranking visiting official presents the awards. This means dress uniforms, customs and courtesies that are given to the visiting official, reading citations of heroic action, pinning a new medal on the uniform, sharp salutes, departure of the official, dismissal of the assembled troops and back to work. Throughout this process, there are no high fives, and it may be weeks after, over a cold beer, that a crew member chooses to recall the event, sometimes admitting—against self-interest—that the mission was really scary.

The author of this book was fortunate to witness this self-effacing quality of Coast Guard heroes at a formal event at the National Air and Space Museum in Washington, D.C. He received a call from VADM Shkor asking for help. The crew of Coast Guard 6031 was to receive the *Aviation Week and Space Technology* Magazine Laureate Award for Operational Excellence, one of the two distinguished awards that was being presented. It was appropriate for a flag officer to introduce the flight crew. Vice Admiral Shkor had a hard calendar conflict and asked the author to "sub" for him. It was a black-tie event. In the Coast Guard, this means mess dress uniform, officially called Dinner Dress Blue Jacket. The keynote speaker for the event was astronaut Buzz Aldrin. Also in attendance was Captain Bob Odom from Coast Guard Air Station Elizabeth City and his wife, Natalie.

The author's aide, LT Rebecca Heatherington, arranged a meeting with the helicopter aircrew a little early so that he could gather enough information to make the best possible introduction. He was surprised by the reaction he received from each of the crew members when they first met. Each was reluctant to be individually recognized. This was not because they did not feel that they "fit in" at this formal event but because they were being singled out for personal recognition. The author feels he probably should have asked if they were enjoying the spotlight, but he could read their faces, and there was no need to ask the question. They were doing this for the Coast Guard not themselves.

Every time the author got near the personal side of things, such as flying in extreme turbulence, lightning and zero visibility, his questions were evaded, and the subject was turned to the operational capabilities of the helicopter or the professionalism of the crew. Having hung around some Coast Guard aviators at Coast Guard Air Station Sacramento as a midgrade officer, the author had learned just enough aviation lingo to get him into trouble. At one point, he asked Dan Molthen about "max gross"—that is, the maximum gross weight of an aircraft at takeoff. Was he worried that putting thirty people into a helicopter designed for ten was an issue? He responded that he had a seventy KT or greater crosswind, incredible power and all the lift he could hope for—again, it was the helicopter.

Shortly after the rescue, LTJG Craig Neubecker received a call from the director of public relations for the *Tiger Alumni News*, a publication that features news from the former students of Cowley County Community College, located in Arkansas City, Kansas. Neubecker had attended Cowley for one year before getting a scholarship to Kansas State University. At the close of the interview, the question was asked: "Do you and your crews consider yourselves heroes?"

> NEUBECKER. *No, I don't consider myself a hero, as we were just doing our job, just like thousands of men and women in the Coast Guard uniform do every day. We just did it under some unusual conditions that got us a lot of attention. The Coast Guard rescues more than four thousand people a year, but you don't hear about most of those rescues unless someone famous is involved, like when JFK Jr. was killed in his plane crash.*
>
> *Although we are a little embarrassed that this rescue has gotten us so much attention, the positive side of it is that it lets the American people see what we do for them.*

Pressed on the issue of exceptionalism, Neubecker, at a later interview, quickly dispelled the notion that they were a special aircrew.

> NEUBECKER. *Look, there were three helicopter aircrews working the* SeaBreeze *SAR case that day. All Coast Guard aircrews train and*

operate to the same high standard; therefore, any of those crews could have and would have done exactly the same thing with exactly the same results. The only difference was that we were the ready helicopter that day, and we got the call—so, we just did what we were trained to do. On a different day, it would have been a different crew; same results with different names.

So, for all of you who wear the Coast Guard uniform and do noble things in dangerous places, your modesty becomes you but never really tells the full story.

14

LOOSE ENDS AND OTHER POSTSCRIPTS

I n the following months, the *SeaBreeze* rescue received an incredible amount of press and media coverage. Members of the aircrew were interviewed by national press and both network and cable television media. On the day after the rescue, ABC and CBS covered this in their first morning segments. Craig Neubecker was interviewed live on CNN's noon news. It was the lead story on *NBC Nightly News*.

The Coast Guard would also take the time to recognize the efforts of those involved. A large awards ceremony was conducted at Air Station Elizabeth City, and it was covered in an article by Captain G. Russell Evans that was later published in the Coast Guard Academy Alumni Association publication, *Bulletin*.[42]

Rescuers Receive Their Due

The impressive awards ceremony for the aviators, rescue swimmers and other air crew members in the dramatic SeaBreeze I *mission was promptly done—exactly one month after the rescue. On a brisk winter morning, January 17, 2001, in a huge hangar at the Coast Guard Air Station, Elizabeth City, NC, the station company in sharp dress blue uniforms assembled for the honors and television cameras. On the dais with Commanding Officer Captain John R. Odom and his staff was Vice Admiral John E. Shkor, Commander of the Coast Guard's Atlantic Area, who presented the awards after his congratulatory remarks. Also present were some hundred guests, military and civilian, and a special congressional delegation. On display were a C-130 Hercules aircraft and one of the Jayhawk helicopters that had packed in twenty-six survivors of the* SeaBreeze I—*very impressive.*

Decorated with Air Medals for the helicopters were LT Daniel Molthen, pilot; LTJG Craig Neubecker, copilot; and Petty Officer Darren Reeves, rescue swimmer—from the first helicopter; and LCDR Randall Watson, pilot; ENS Steven Bonn, copilot; and Petty Officer Robert Florisi, rescue swimmer—from the second helicopter. The air crews of the first C-130, on-scene Commander were also decorated as follows CDR Charles Holman, CG Commendation Medal; LT Eric Storch, CG Achievement Medal; Petty Officer Lorne Green, Air Medal; Petty Officer Samuel Pulliam, Air Medal; Petty Officer Omar Acuna, CG Achievement Medal; Petty Officer Eric Benson, CG Achievement Medal; Petty Officer Sean Fuller, CG Achievement Medal; Petty Officer Donald Welch, CG Achievement Medal; Petty Officer Edward Vickery, CG Achievement Medal; and Petty Officer Jimmy Barr, Commandant's Letter of Commendation.

Before closing the awards ceremony, VADM Shkor added an important note to others who served at the Air Station:

Beyond the professionalism, beyond the heroism, there is something I think makes today's ceremony quite special. I would call it teamwork. It is the inspiring performance of the entire Elizabeth City team; the pilots, the aircrews, the rescue swimmers and the maintenance folks. They are often the unsung heroes.

This one unit generated five aircraft sorties to respond to the SeaBreeze I *within an hour. That's marvelous. That's a credit undeniably that runs to you who keep these planes in the air.*

Coast Guard Chaplain (on loan from the U.S. Navy Chaplain Corps) LT Alan Andraeas provided the benediction: "Through their heroic deeds of sacrifice, by risking everything to save others, by snatching life back out of the jaws of death…[they brought] back those who were lost and perishing."

Perhaps as a result of the earlier "skepticism" of District staff, a special award was created, the Order of the Silver Clicker, signed by VADM Shkor and presented to the crew of the first helicopter. Each of the attached "clickers" displayed the number twenty-six. All four of the aircrew still have their copies.

Photograph courtesy of Darren Reeves.

For several weeks after the rescue, letters of appreciation arrived at Coast Guard Air Station Elizabeth City. Bob Odom commented:

> ODOM. *They were addressed to me, but each one expressed their gratitude and sometimes amazement of the professionalism and bravery of our air crews. I made special efforts to share these with all of our Air Station personnel. It was about them, and I wanted them to know it.*

The rescue got the attention of Secretary of Defense Bill Cohen, who felt moved to express his appreciation.

The crew of CG6031 was recognized by nearly every major aviation organization that year for their heroic actions. They first traveled to Anaheim, California, to be formally recognized by the Helicopter Association International (HAI), the world's largest helicopter organization, at their Heli-Expo Salute to Excellence for the most outstanding operational use of a helicopter. They were then off to Washington, D.C., to be recognized by the American Helicopter Society (AHS) at their annual symposium for the top rescue of the year. The crew then traveled back to the West Coast to San Diego, California, to be recognized by *Rotor & Wing* magazine for conducting the most dangerous and dramatic rescue of the year. The crew was also nationally recognized by the Coast Guard at the Annual Coast Guard Foundation Dinner Awards, which were held in New York City that year.

As mentioned earlier, Coast Guard Headquarters in Washington, D.C., issued a media advisory listing the "Top Rescues of the Century." The advisory cited the *SeaBreeze* mission as the "greatest rescue," stating, "Coast Guard Air Station Elizabeth City, North Carolina, performed one of the most heroic rescues in Coast Guard history on December 17, 2000."

THE SECRETARY OF DEFENSE
WASHINGTON

January 19, 2001

Captain Robert Odom, USCG
Commanding Officer
U.S. Coast Guard Air Station
Elizabeth City, NJ 27909-5004

Dear Captain Odom:

I have read the chilling accounts of the December 17 U.S. Coast Guard rescue of the crew of SeaBreeze I off the Virginia coast last month. I want to commend the men and women in your command who risked their own lives to bring the 32 crew members to safety.

This daring rescue was a great testament to the training and readiness of those who serve the United States Coast Guard. You and your team have given us another reason to be tremendously proud of their service and I want to extend my congratulations and my thanks to all those who were involved in the rescue.

With deep appreciation and best wishes, I am

Sincerely,

CC: The Master Chief Petty Officer of the Coast Guard

Image courtesy of Bob Odom.

Also discussed earlier, in April 2001, the aircrew of CG 6031 was chosen to receive the *Aviation Week and Space Technology* Magazine Laureate Award of Operational Excellence. But there is more. The crew of CG6031 was inducted into the Aviation Laureates Hall of Fame. Their names would be next to the likes of previous honorees, such as Chuck Yeager and Neil Armstrong. The awards ceremony was held after visiting hours at the Smithsonian's Air and Space Museum as part of a formal (black-tie) dinner

AMT2 Lorne Green (*second from left*), AST1 Darren Reeves (*third from left*), LTJG Craig Neubecker (*third from right*) and Lieutenant Dan Molthen (*second from right*). *Photograph courtesy of* Aviation Week and Space Technology *Magazine.*

in the shadow of the Wright Flyer. Introductions and presentations for various awards were made by individuals representing various organizations and included astronaut Buzz Aldrin.

While receiving this prestigious award at a formal event would normally be an occasion to celebrate, this event presented an unforeseen problem that is integral to this story. The Coast Guard and other military services require a basic wardrobe of uniforms for each service member. The "uniform of the day" is specified by the command, and it must be one of those basic uniforms. Junior enlisted members are not required to have the Dinner Dress Blue Jacket (the military equivalent of a civilian tuxedo), and few, because of the expense, purchase the uniform until they progress to higher rates. Such was the case for AMT2 Lorne Green.

In the unscripted, traditional sense of Coast Guard family, fellow aviators jumped in to assist. LT Eric Storch (copilot of CG 1504) had an old dinner dress uniform and willingly donated it to the cause. LT Molthen and LTJG Neubecker chipped in to have the uniform tailored and provided insignias and dress medals as required. When AMT2 Green arrived at the formal dinner, he and the rest of the aircrew made an impressive appearance as a cohesive flight crew—all in the same, spiffy uniform.

THE SIKORSKY CORPORATION ALSO used the event to promote the H-60 as the preeminent rescue helicopter. In the company's press release dated May 15, 2001, it provided a Coast Guard photo of CG 6031 conducting hoist operations and a wave spike driving up the port side of *SeaBreeze*. The press release stated, "On scene, the seas were running thirty feet or more, lashing the ship's deck and, at times, dousing the helicopters with saltwater as survivors were hoisted aboard."[43] Although rare, this wave spike phenomena can be deadly. Open-ocean waves impacting a ship's hull at right angles, or nearly so, can violently explode upward to expend their energy. Waves hitting a grounded ship undergo somewhat different dynamics, making them potentially even more explosive. As a result, some rescue operations do not end well.

Almost three years to the day after the *SeaBreeze* rescue, two HH-60 helicopters from Coast Guard Air Station Kodiak, Alaska, responded to a vessel in distress near Unalaska Island. The *Selendang Ayu*, a bulk carrier, had lost power and was drifting to shore. In conjunction with Coast Guard Cutter *Alex Haley* and its embarked HH-65 Dolphin helicopter, evacuation of the crew began. After several hoists, all but seven officers and one deck cadet remained aboard the ship. In one of the last sorties, one of the Kodiak helicopters hoisted six of the remaining seven crewmembers, leaving its rescue swimmer and the ship's captain behind. That helicopter was CG 6020. The Aircraft Commander was LCDR Dave Neel.

> NEEL. *The two H-60s hoisted eighteen of the twenty-six crew. Then a large wave broke on the grounded ship's bow, ejecting water up and over the helicopter, flaming out the engines. The accident board determined we were at 102' AGL* [above ground/water level] *when the event occurred.*

The rush of seawater was so intensive that the helicopter lost all power and crashed into the water below. CGC *Haley*'s HH-65 was able to rescue three of the helicopter crew and one of the ship's crew who had been hoisted earlier. The other five men were never found.

⌐•⌐

THE ISSUE OF "OVERLOADING" CG 6031 with thirty people (the four aircrew plus the twenty-six survivors) was raised several times following the mission. Craig Neubecker, once a contract maintenance test pilot at NAS Whiting Field, Florida, took the time to address the question after retirement.

NEUBECKER. *For most Sikorsky H-60 variants, such as the Black Hawk, the Seahawk and the Pave Hawk, the maximum gross weight of the aircraft is 23,500 pounds. The Jayhawk, however, has a lower maximum gross weight of only 21,884 pounds. This is due to the asymmetrical configuration of the 120-gallon external tanks on the left side of the aircraft that can put the Jayhawk out of center of gravity limitations above 21,884 pounds. Therefore, the Jayhawk has a lower max gross weight than other H-60 variants.*

There were no scales used that day, so all weights are estimations, but during the SeaBreeze *mission, CG 6031 was fully fueled with three 120-gallon external tanks and a crew of four. That put the takeoff gross weight at approximately 21,860 pounds, or just under max gross weight. The aircraft burns 1,200 pounds of fuel per hour, so for the one-and-a-half-hour transit to scene, 6031 burned off 1,800 pounds of fuel, bringing the gross weight down to roughly 20,060 pounds. The aircraft then burned off about another four hundred pounds of fuel during the twenty minutes spent on scene preparing and hoisting the survivors, bringing the gross weight down to about 19,660 pounds.*

The twenty-six survivors hoisted from the SeaBreeze *were mostly Greek, Indonesians and Filipinos—smaller men by American standards, weighing approximately 150 pounds each, but each of them also brought along a suitcase or bag containing whatever worldly possession they wanted to save, as well as being dressed in heavy clothes, coats and bulky lifejackets, so each most likely weighed about 160 pounds. Therefore, using the 160 pound per man average, the twenty-six survivors weighed a total of approximately 4,160 pounds. Adding that survivor weight to the aircraft meant that CG6031 weighed approximately 23,820 pounds with the survivors onboard. So, most likely, the aircraft was approximately 1,936 pounds—nearly a ton, over maximum gross weight leaving the scene of the rescue.*

This resulted in a lot of "Monday morning quarterbacking" following the rescue but was and is completely in line with the Coast Guard Air Operations Manual regulations, which state:

"D.2.b. (1) Saving Human Life

If a mission is likely to save human life, it warrants a maximum effort. When no suitable alternatives exist and the mission has a reasonable chance of success, the risk of damage or abuse of the aircraft is acceptable, even though such damage or abuse may render the aircraft unrecoverable."

Air Station Elizabeth City Commanding Officer Captain Bob Odom also provided top cover for the crew of CG 6031 to the naysayers and stated that a seasoned helo pilot knows "instinctively" when his helo is too heavy to fly, and this crew knew that, while the aircraft was probably technically overloaded, they also knew that, under the circumstances, the risk was warranted to save those lives and that the Jayhawk could handle it under the weather conditions they faced with the high winds that helped the helicopter's hover performance.

On a side note—to all those Monday morning quarterbacks, if each of the helicopters had only rescued seventeen survivors each [the original plan]*, each helicopter would have still been well over maximum gross weight. Seventeen survivors would have weighed approximately 2,720 pounds, added to the 19,660 aircraft weight; it would have put each aircraft at about 22,380 pounds, still well over the 21,884 pounds maximum gross weight of the Jayhawk.*[44]

The fact that the crew of CG 6031 successfully rescued twenty-six survivors while not damaging the aircraft, despite being overloaded, and dealing with systems malfunctions and flying in extreme weather conditions is a testament to their training, skills and dedication that resulted in their heroic actions.

To THE WET, SCARED and exhausted person who is rescued from the grips of the sea, there is little concern about where the pilot learned to fly. However, within the Coast Guard aviation community, you will find a wide spectrum of commission sources, not just the Coast Guard. The Coast Guard offers the Direct Commission Aviator Program, but one does not necessarily transfer from another service at their current service rank. For instance, a warrant officer through O-1 would transfer over as an ensign. An O-2 and above would normally be commissioned as a lieutenant junior grade. junior officer pilots, who are selected through the Direct Commission Aviator Program, exchange their prior uniform for Coast Guard blues.

There are many reasons pilots from other services transfer to the Coast Guard. These reasons include spending more time with family (as opposed to long overseas deployments), more challenging flying conditions (on-the-deck flying with no horizon), more flying opportunities and, of course, a true commitment to serve and save lives.

These pilots make a special sacrifice to enter the Coast Guard. Competition for openings varies but is ever-present; approximately 60 percent of those who are successfully screened will be selected.

In the *SeaBreeze* rescue, there were ten pilots. Only half earned their wings with the Coast Guard.

LT Dan Molthen, prior U.S. Navy pilot
LTJG Craig Neubecker, prior U.S. Army pilot
LCDR Randall Watson, prior U.S. Army pilot
ENS Steve Bonn, prior U.S. Army pilot
CDR Charlie Holman, U.S. Coast Guard pilot
LT Eric Storch, U.S. Coast Guard pilot
LCDR John Keeton, prior U.S. Army pilot
LT Kristina Ahman, U.S. Coast Guard pilot
LT Mark Ward, U.S. Coast Guard pilot
CDR Rod Ansley, U.S. Coast Guard pilot

THE ABILITY TO LAUNCH three helicopters and two C-130 aircraft in less than an hour is, in itself, a remarkable accomplishment, especially when one or more helicopters are down for maintenance. As part of the research phase in the development of *On the Wings of Angels*, Eric Storch provided sections of the "aviation staffing standard model," which addresses the issue of helicopter availability. "The model provides three helicopters, assuming that each has 71 percent availability, to give a statistical probability of having one aircraft available for SAR response 98 percent of the time, two helicopters available 80 percent of the time, and all three available only 36 percent of the time."

Mark Ward, the pilot in command of the third helicopter (CG 6026), also commented on this feat.

WARD. *I was the Engineering Officer at the time, and I remember the all-hands-on-deck scramble to get the third aircraft in the air. Coast Guard aviation maintenance is the best in the world—hands down. I can say that unconditionally from my nine years of experience at Sikorsky. Launching all three helicopters in less than an hour on a Sunday afternoon speaks directly to the superior professionalism, skill and attitude of the men and women of the Air Station E. City hangar deck. They make it all possible.*

<hr/>

SITE RESEARCH WAS CRITICAL to understanding the many nuances of this story. While visiting Coast Guard Air Station Elizabeth City, the author viewed the cabin and cockpit spaces of the MH-60J to fully understand the difficulty in packing thirty people into an area designed for ten. There are 130 inches between the instrument panel in front of the pilots and the aft cabin wall. The cabin width is 74 inches. Some of this space is already taken by rescue equipment, fixed seating and avionics. This is comparable to a typical full-size SUV, which is slightly longer in length and slightly smaller in width.

<hr/>

FOLLOWING THE SINKING OF *SeaBreeze*, the internet was awash with speculation about the *SeaBreeze*'s casualty. Many questions still remain unanswered. Due to its distance offshore, any marine casualty investigation was to be conducted by authorities of the country of registry, Panama. Vessel casualty investigation reports are filed with the International Maritime Organization (IMO), an agency of the United Nations. To date, there is no investigative report filed with the IMO about the sinking of the *SeaBreeze*. If the ultimate fate of the *SeaBreeze* was to be a final voyage to the ship breakers, it avoided their acetylene knives and rests comfortably in Davy Jones's Locker in about 4,300 feet of water, 270 miles off of the Virginia coast.

<hr/>

AFTER THE *SEABREEZE* SANK, Captain Solon Papadopoulos filed a lawsuit against the ship's owners, Cruise Ventures Three Corporation, asserting that, as a result of the traumatic incident, he was injured and sought compensation. The trial court did not agree, and the case was appealed to Florida's Third District Court of Appeal. That court released its findings on September 19, 2007.

Captain Solon M. Papadopoulos "Papadopoulos", the plaintiff below, appeals a final order issued by the trial court, dismissing his negligence action against Cruise Ventures Three Corp., International Shipping Partners Inc., and DLJ Capital Funding Inc. (collectively "the defendants"). We affirm.

Papadopoulos, a seaman, claims he was injured when the vessel he was working on encountered a severe storm and strong winds on December 17, 2000, resulting in the ship taking on water and in a U.S. Coast Guard rescue of those on board. The ship ultimately sank.

Papadopoulos claimed that, as a result of this experience, he developed post-traumatic stress disorder and leukemia. In answers to interrogatories propounded by the defendants, Papadopoulos stated that, prior to the subject accident, he was both medically and physically fit; was not taking any medicine or drugs; and denied being diagnosed and/or receiving any treatment for any of the ailments described in Dr. Karianakis's report. Dr. Karianakis, a hematologist, was treating Papadopoulos for hairy cell leukemia. Additionally, Papadopoulos testified under oath in his deposition that he had not been treated for leukemia prior to the subject accident.

When Papadopoulos was questioned during his deposition regarding any pre-incident pension/disability litigation, he testified that he had never been involved in any litigation; he had not applied for nor received any disability benefits in Greece, his native country; and that he had not received any pension benefits in Greece.

An investigation performed by the defendants, however, revealed that, prior to the subject accident, in December 2000, Papadopoulos had engaged in litigation in Greece regarding work-related injuries he sustained in 1995; he was diagnosed with hairy cell leukemia on November 4, 1995; and he was awarded a pension beginning on January 1, 1996, based upon a medical opinion finding that he was sixty-seven percent disabled. The litigation in Greece continued for years and involved protracted litigation and appeals that were ongoing during the instant litigation.

Based upon the ample record before us, we find that the trial court did not abuse its discretion in dismissing Papadopoulos's lawsuit.

We entirely agree with the trial court that Papadopoulos has forfeited his right to seek redress from his claimed injuries based upon his material misrepresentations and omissions that go to the heart of his claims. We, therefore, affirm the trial court's order dismissing Papadopoulos's negligence action.

Affirmed.
ROTHENBERG, Judge.

ALMOST ALL OF THE critical players in the *SeaBreeze* rescue have retired from the Coast Guard, moved away and are doing other things. During the research phase of writing *On the Wings of Angels*, many of the pilots and aircrew were asking about the others who flew that mission, their whereabouts and contact information. While conducting a personal interview with ASTC Robert "Bob" Florisi, he went a step further and said, "We really need to have a *SeaBreeze* rescue reunion."

Front row, from left to right: Charles Holman, Captain Eric Storch, Darren Reeves, Lorne Green (*with an actual lifejacket that was left in the helicopter by a* SeaBreeze *crewman*), Bob Odom, Steve Bonn and Carl Moore (author). *Second row*: Craig Neubecker, Dan Molthen, Rod Ansley and ASTC Bob Florisi. Missing is Randy Watson (*see memoriam*). *Cindy Moore photograph.*

On September 23, 2017, in Hangar 7 (the club) at Coast Guard Air Station Elizabeth City, most of the pilots and aircrew and their wives attended a dinner to commemorate the rescue that had occurred almost seventeen years earlier.

In 2006, *Virginia Living* magazine published an article about the heroic *SeaBreeze* mission. The article was written by Jake Denton. The magazine was looking for an illustration for the cover page and engaged the services of artist Rick Farrell. Rick was given three photographs taken by Steve Bonn (see chapter 11) from a disposable Kodak camera. From these three, Rick was able to render an incredibly accurate scene in oil. The artwork was reproduced in full-size canvas print for each person attending the reunion. The artwork has found its way to other places, including the Coast Guard Training Center in Cape May, New Jersey, and the cover of this book.

———————

As THE FIRST DRAFT of the manuscript for *On the Wings of Angels* neared completion, Captain Bob Odom revealed that he had a long-standing concern that the Coast Guard awards process did not adequately acknowledge the efforts put forth by those who were directly involved in the *SeaBreeze* rescue. While all of the helicopter crews for CG 6031 and CG 6001 were awarded the Coast Guard Air Medal for their efforts, Odom felt that the Coast Guard should have awarded a higher award, the Coast Guard Distinguished Flying Cross.

> ODOM. *If there ever was a case that warranted the issuance of a DFC, this is it.*

The author of this book agreed that it was incongruous for the Coast Guard to claim the *SeaBreeze* rescue to be the "greatest rescue of the century" and not issue its highest aviation award to even some of those who flew the mission. Both men independently contacted the Coast Guard Vice Commandant Admiral Charles Michel with supportive material to ask for a review. It was nine months before they received a reply. By then, the Coast Guard had a new commandant and a new vice commandant.

In a letter dated November 19, 2018, Admiral Charles Ray, Vice Commandant, replied:

Dear Admiral Moore,

Thank you for your request to review and reconsider the level of recognition for the Coast Guard personnel involved in the search and rescue case of the M/V Sea Breeze I, which took place on December 17, 2000.

Upon receiving your letter, my predecessor, Admiral Michel, directed the Atlantic Area and Headquarters Awards Boards to review these awards using the information you provided, plus any additional information they could discover. Both awards boards exhaustively reviewed this material and determined there is not any new information which would warrant a change in the levels of recognition awarded to the members involved in this case.

Nothing in this review should diminish the courageous actions and initiative taken by these Coast Guard members in carrying out this historic Coast Guard rescue. Unfortunately, there is just not sufficient new information that would warrant overturning the judgment of the awards board convened in 2000.

I appreciate your patience while we researched and reviewed the details of this historic case.

———

Due to the exigency recognized by the aircrew of Rescue 6031 and the panic displayed by the crew of the *SeaBreeze*, rescue swimmer Darren Reeves informed the helicopter crew that he was going to load two people into the rescue basket at a time

Everyone involved then realized the extreme urgency of the situation and the necessity of getting all of the people off of the ship as fast as humanly possible. No one knew how long the ship could stay afloat.

> Reeves. *I thought we could hoist two at a time. The hoist can lift six hundred, and two people don't weigh that much.*

He chose two of the *SeaBreeze* crewmen to get into the basket.

At the time, there was only one other well-publicized Coast Guard rescue in which two people were placed in the rescue basket, the *Marine Flower II* rescue, which was also flown by Dan Molthen (for this rescue, he received the Coast Guard Distinguished Flying Cross medal). However, unlike the

SeaBreeze rescue, in which all the people who were hoisted were adults, the *Marine Flower II* involved a mother and an infant.

Several years after the *SeaBreeze* rescue, the idea of hoisting two at a time would get more attention.

The Coast Guard Research and Development Center (RDC), located in New London, Connecticut, is the Coast Guard's primary facility performing research, development and tests and evaluation in support of the service's major missions, including search and rescue. "In 2009, the Research and Development Center (RDC) conducted an internal Coast Guard study," said M.J. Lewandowski, a research project manager for the RDC. "The study noted that the Coast Guard's ability to respond to mass rescue incidents was, and still is, somewhat limited in the methods available to remove large numbers of people from a hazardous marine situation quickly and safely."

Coast Guard Academy mechanical engineering cadets have been prototyping a new and improved rescue basket, which could revolutionize the way the Coast Guard conducts search and rescue missions on board the MH-60 Jayhawk helicopters. First Class Cadets Christian Breviario, Riely Brande, Benjamin Crutchfield, Nolan Richerson and Spencer Smith spent their last year working closely with the RDC to improve on the current rescue basket design after receiving input from search and rescue operators in the fleet.

The RDC and academy leadership approached Breviario and his capstone group at the beginning of their senior year to see if an improvement could be made to the current design, which would increase the Coast Guard's effectiveness during mass rescue incidents. Breviario said:

> *We have added a means of entry that is easier for people who may be injured or have limited mobility. We have also maximized the space dimensions of the basket, given the dimensions of the MH-60 Jayhawk cabin. With these modifications, we have made the basket more accessible, decreased the amount of time needed per hoisting evolution and improved upon the effectiveness of the Coast Guard during mass rescue incidents.*

The new design, which is roomy enough for two individuals to comfortably sit in the basket, allows Coast Guard operators to shave off precious time during mass rescue situations. During mass rescue scenarios in which eighteen or more victims require helicopter assistance, the cadets have determined that the new basket could cut the time required to get everyone hoisted by half.

Cutting down on the time required for Coast Guard rescue operations by adding a means of entry and increasing the dimensions were not the only alterations the cadets made to the rescue basket. They also reconfigured the flotation system of the basket, which increased the buoyancy of the basket by seventy-nine pounds of force. This upgrade will also allow for the increased comfort of victims within the basket, as they will be surrounded by buoyant material on all sides.

Breviario hopes to see the design implemented into the fleet as the new standard rescue basket used in Coast Guard operations. The capstone group is currently pursuing a patent for their design and waiting on the RDC to decide if they are interested in further testing.[45]

15

REFLECTIONS

"Sane Aviators Do Not Fly into Such Weather"

After a week of intense media attention and other disruptions, the Air Station resumed its normal cadence of OPTEMPO. This is the continuance of ongoing and never-ending training, scheduled and unscheduled flight operations, essential aircraft maintenance and the necessary administration that goes into managing a small corporation. On December 27, CDR Charlie Holman wrote a memorandum about the rescue operation to LCDR Paul Lange, the Administration Officer and Safety Officer at the Air Station. The memorandum recounted the operation from his viewpoint as the Senior Duty Officer. In addition to the timeline of events, he included a summary of "factors" he felt were important to include in his report.

FACTORS IN THE CASE

Weather

An Elizabeth City C-130 D5 law enforcement and "First Flight Fly-By" mission commemorating the anniversary of the Wright brothers' historic first flight were both canceled due to adverse weather. A USAF four-star General, who was scheduled to arrive at Elizabeth City on Sunday morning, orbited overhead prior to continuing on to the alternate airfield because his itinerary had been cancelled, also due to severe weather. At the time, Elizabeth City's weather included thunderstorms in the vicinity, and conditions were favorable for tornadoes. Elizabeth City fell within the southern portion of a weather warning area issued by the National Weather Service. Two hours later, the system pushed through and sat offshore. Elizabeth City launched five aircraft and crews, all of which penetrated thunderstorms to arrive on-scene.

The turbulence was enough to cause three of the crewmembers on CG 1504 to get physically sick throughout the mission. The turbulence provided a considerable hazard to personnel in the cargo compartment, who were, at times, unstrapped to conduct aircraft safety checks [and] *configure the aircraft for equipment drops. Airdrops of survival equipment would have been executable but extremely risky.*

Communications

Communications on UHF and VHF-FM were busy. The radio operator, navigator and both pilots shared in communications with surface vessels, company aircraft, the distress vessel, CAMSLANT Chesapeake, Air Station Elizabeth City and LANTAREA via phone patch. HF frequency communications were very poor. We attempted to relay case status on numerous occasions. Much of my effort was involved keeping the aircraft flying in the turbulent weather.

Safety

TCAS was inoperative. CG 1504 had an inoperable TCAS, and no radar coverage for aircraft separation was available. Air-to-air TACAN only allowed distance tracking for one of the five known aircraft in the vicinity. Five Coast Guard aircraft and aircrews flew into known severe weather, weather that was usually avoided by at least twenty NMs in order to provide assistance to mariners. These aircrews risked their lives and the aircraft they were flying; both were flown to operational and personal endurance limits.

In Retrospect

The Coast Guard was extremely lucky that day. All of the ingredients were ripe for a disastrous outcome, both for the mariners on board the vessel and the rescuers. Sane aviators do not fly into such weather. Aircrews usually navigate around such systems. All of the aircraft attempted to circumnavigate the weather, but to no avail. They remained focused on reaching the distressed vessel. Major thunderstorms have been known to rip wings off aircraft from "updrafts" and also drive aircraft into the ground from tremendous "micro-burst" downdrafts. All of the aircraft took considerable risk.

If you changed any factor on this case, the outcome would not have been as successful. Had it been nighttime; had they delayed two hours, the weather would have been overhead the vessel; had the survivors not spoken English; had the freezing level been at the surface, icing would have greatly hindered passage to the vessel, and aircraft deicing systems would have robbed precious fuel; had the survivors been in rafts, lifeboats or, worse, in the water, excessive time required to hoist all survivors would have eaten into fuel reserves. People would have been left behind. Every action was executed like a precision timepiece, the mission was picture perfect.

God had mercy on the Coast Guard, and the survivors, that day.

Respectfully submitted/
CDR C. W. HOLMAN, USCG
12/27/00

ACKNOWLEDGEMENTS

Throughout the research phase of this project, I was fortunate to meet many of the people who participated in the *SeaBreeze* rescue mission. Some, at the time, felt that there might be a story to be told at a later time and saved articles, video tapes and mementoes of the rescue.

CRAIG NEUBECKER

Craig had the collateral duty as the Command Public Affairs Officer at Coast Guard Air Station Elizabeth City and provided a wealth of material to aid in the research. He graciously reviewed many chapters of the draft manuscript to ensure accuracy. I had the opportunity to meet with him, his wife, Kimberly, and their two children in their Florida home. Craig had just finished reviewing the chapter on Kill Devil Hills when he told me about his personal connection to the Kill Devil Hills monument.

When Craig met Kim, she was serving in the Coast Guard at the U.S. Coast Guard Training Center in Yorktown, Virginia. They fell in love. Craig, in a move to "seal the deal," decided to invite Kim to fly with him to Kill Devil Hills and see the Wright Brothers Memorial. On Sunday, February 14, 1999, Valentine's Day, Craig rented a small plane, and they headed south to the North Carolina Coast. The weather was "iffy," and there was enough turbulence to get Kim airsick. Once they arrived at First Flight Airport, Craig took Kim to the memorial and, next, to the statue of Orville Wright, where, on bended knee, he proposed to Kim. They later had two lovely children and gave their son the middle name Orville.

Craig retired as a commander after twenty-three years of combined Army and Coast Guard service. He logged over six thousand hours flying air assault and medevac missions for the Army, completed a joint tour with the Navy as an instructor pilot and was a plank owner of the Coast Guard's Helicopter Interdiction Tactical Squadron (HITRON). There, he flew armed counterdrug and Homeland Security missions, in addition to flying SAR missions from Elizabeth City to Kodiak, Alaska. Craig retired with two Coast Guard Air Medals and many other awards. He continues to fly helicopters for a national air ambulance service.

Dan Molthen

Dan retired after thirty-three years of military service, having logged over 7,500 hours flying for the Navy and the Coast Guard. He is, perhaps, one of the most decorated Coast Guard helicopter pilots, having been awarded the Distinguished Flying Cross twice, the Coast Guard Air Medal twice and many others. Prior to his retirement, he was involved in the filming of the movie *The Guardian*, both as a technical advisor and an on-camera actor, depicting an H-60 helicopter pilot.

Dan's retirement ceremony was held in a hangar at Coast Guard Air Station Elizabeth City. The guest speaker at the retirement ceremony was Captain Jim O'Keefe, Dan's close friend and colleague. He said,

> *There are two words that I would use to describe Dan, heroic and noble. He is the most humble and genuine person I know and epitomizes the word noble to me.*

During an interview with the media the day following the rescue, Dan told a reporter that he had the best job in the world.

> *We do have the best job in the world. We get to rescue people, but not only that, I get out of the helicopter to meet them as they come out, see their appreciation and sometimes relief that they are now safe. There's that human connection that is so real, and really rewarding. Yes, we have the best job in the world. What better thing is there?*

Dan is currently retired and living with his wife, Theresa, in the Daytona Beach, Florida area. They have three children. Their daughter Erin is married to a Coast Guard helicopter pilot who is stationed in Mobile, Alabama.

DARREN REEVES

Darren brings a certain presence to any room he occupies. I left our first interview with even more respect for those who leave the safety of a helicopter to rescue those in imminent peril. Darren was a member of one of the first waves of new rescue swimmers to serve the Coast Guard. After five years of service in the U.S. Army, he spent twenty-five years in the Coast Guard.

After his first tour at Coast Guard Air Station Elizabeth City, he was advanced to chief petty officer and transferred for duty to San Diego, only to return to "E City" as a rescue swimmer instructor. After making senior chief, he returned to the Air Station Elizabeth City in an operational billet.

He retired from the Coast Guard in January 2012, after logging over 2,200 hours of flight time. While in the Coast Guard, he received three Air Medals, three Commendation Medals, four Achievement Medals and two Letters of Commendation on rescue missions.

He and his wife, Rhoda, have two sons serving in the U.S. Marine Corps, a daughter and son in college and two sons at home.

He currently works as a trainer, developing curriculum and working with the development team to implement the system known as Coast Guard Logistics Information Management System to replace the current system.

STEVE BONN

Steve retired as a lieutenant commander in 2014 after twenty-three years of combined service with the Army and Coast Guard. He logged over 5,200 flight hours and was awarded the Air Medal four times. He served in Kodiak, Alaska, and Elizabeth City, North Carolina.

The SeaBreeze *rescue was a unique introduction to the Coast Guard for me. I had only been in the Coast Guard for four months since transferring from the Army. This was only my third SAR case but the first one that involved actually rescuing people. The two prior were just uneventful searches. For our efforts, we were awarded the Air Medal for the* SeaBreeze *rescue. Everyone is hopeful to receive this award just once in their career, and it was unreal to receive this after my first real SAR case.*

Seven months after the *SeaBreeze* rescue, Steve tragically lost his young wife, Lisa, the mother of their two children, to cancer.

It was very fortunate that I had switched to the Coast Guard before she passed. The Coast Guard was able to support our family and allow flexibility in my schedule to adjust to being a single parent with young children that I could not have done in the Army. Even though I did have all of the responsibility of caring for them myself in the beginning, I did remarry while the kids were still very young. I have given credit to Mary anytime I have the opportunity that she wound up having a greater influence on what they achieved than what I would ever have been able to do by myself. Unfortunately, our marriage did not last.

Steve's two children are now young adults. His daughter recently graduated from the University of North Carolina in Chapel Hill, and his son graduated from the Naval Academy and is currently serving as a pilot in the Navy.

After his retirement, Steve again married and currently lives in Elizabeth City, North Carolina, with his wife, Jill, and her two children. He is a medical helicopter pilot for a hospital in North Carolina.

A recent photograph of Steve Bonn (*left*) and Senior Chief Bob Florisi (*right*) in front of H-60, which was painted in a special color to commemorate the centennial anniversary of coast guard aviation. *Photograph courtesy of Steve Bonn.*

ROBERT FLORISI

Chief Warrant Officer Florisi remains on active duty and is stationed in New Orleans; there, he is tasked with inspecting offshore drilling rigs. Over his career, he has served at Coast Guard Air Station Elizabeth City; North Bend, Oregon; Corpus Christi, Texas; and Mobile, Alabama, and he has been a STAN team member at the Aviation Training Center. The mission of the rescue swimmer STAN team is to provide rescue swimmer standardization to the MH-65 and MH-60 communities. Florisi has been stationed at Elizabeth City twice. Most recently, he headed up the aviation survival technician (rescue swimmer) shop at the Air Station in Elizabeth City. In his twenty-three years of service as an aviation survival technician, he logged over two thousand hours of flight time and has been directly involved in rescue operations and medevacs. He was awarded the Air Medal for the *SeaBreeze* rescue and has many other operational awards of excellence. He says that he is a Texan by heart, and after retirement, he plans to move to Texas with his wife, Sunni.

CHARLES HOLMAN

Charlie retired after twenty-four years with the U.S. Coast Guard. During the *SeaBreeze* rescue, Charlie was the Aviation Engineering Officer assigned to Coast Guard Air Station Elizabeth City. In addition to his engineering department head responsibility, Charlie volunteered to stand search and rescue duty and was an instructor pilot and senior flight examiner in the HC-130 Hercules aircraft.

Charlie started his Coast Guard career training Coast Guard reserve forces in the Fifth Coast Guard District in Portsmouth, Virginia. He entered U.S. Navy Flight School in 1981 and commenced his Coast Guard aviation career. He has logged over six thousand flight hours in Coast Guard HC-130B, E and H model aircraft and has executed over one hundred search and rescue cases. He has been assigned to Air Stations Clearwater, Florida; Barbers Point, Hawaii; and Elizabeth City, North Carolina. He completed a staff tour at Coast Guard headquarters as the C-130 and Gulfstream aircraft systems manager, and he finished his operational career at Air Station Elizabeth City. After retiring from active duty, he worked as a contractor at the Coast Guard Aviation Logistics Center in Elizabeth City, North Carolina, supporting the service life upgrade and systems improvements to the Coast Guard MH-65D rescue helicopter.

Charlie is the third "coastie" in his family; two of his uncles served in the Coast Guard. One uncle piloted Navy landing craft, carrying ground troops to Omaha Beach during the Normandy invasion of World War II. His immediate family boasts mariners in the U.S. Navy and U.S. Merchant Marine. Charlie "broke" the seafaring tradition and pursued aviation.

Charlie resides in Chesapeake, Virginia, with his wife of forty-three years, April. They have two sons, who are both married, and three grandchildren.

RADM TIM RIKER

In uniform, Tim was a contemporary colleague of mine, and after retirement, he remains a close personal friend. Following his devotion to his family, especially his wife, Miriam, the United States Coast Guard is in a close second place of importance. He is also a well-read student of early American history, generally, and Coast Guard history, specifically. As the early chapters of *On the Wings of Angels* emerged from my home printer, I realized that Tim would be the perfect person to review the manuscript. I feel truly honored that he assisted with this project.

CAPTAIN BOB ODOM

One of the most challenging parts of the research phase was locating the men and women who were "material witnesses" to the *SeaBreeze* event. Late in this process, I located the commanding officer of Coast Guard Air Station Elizabeth City who left church on rescue day to go into the Air Station to oversee this incredible rescue operation. Bob took a very special interest in the effort to tell this important Coast Guard story and provided material that had not yet been uncovered by months of research. He helped me contact his Executive Officer Captain Rod Ansley and Operations Officer Commander Joe Seebald for their input. More importantly, Bob agreed to review the manuscript as part of a larger effort to get the story right.

Bob is a 1966 graduate of the Virginia Military Institute. He began his military career as a Marine Corps aviator and served as an H-46 helicopter pilot in Vietnam from May 1968 until May 1969, where he logged over eight hundred flight hours. He subsequently transitioned to KC-130s for the remaining three years of his nearly seven and a half years as a marine.

In June 1975, Bob entered the Coast Guard as a direct commission aviator and was stationed as a HC-130 duty standing pilot at Coast Guard Air Station Elizabeth City, North Carolina. His subsequent tours included Coast Guard Air Stations Sacramento, California; Kodiak, Alaska; Clearwater, Florida; and, again, at Elizabeth City, North Carolina, as the operations officer and, later, as the commanding officer. Additionally, he had two tours as a Coast Guard exchange C-130 pilot with the U.S. Air Force at McChord AFB, Washington, and RAF Woodbridge, United Kingdom. Bob retired from Air Station Elizabeth City as a captain in June 2001, having completed some twenty-six years in the Coast Guard for a combined active duty time of thirty-three and a half years. He logged approximately nine thousand flight hours during his military career.

Both of Bob's parents served as Coast Guard officers during World War II. Bob married Natalie Gregory in April 1967. They currently reside in Waynesboro, Virginia (Shenandoah Valley). They have two daughters, five granddaughters and one grandson.

CAPTAIN ERIC STORCH

Eric is a 1994 graduate of The Citadel. He began his Coast Guard career as the officer in charge of the U.S. Coast Guard Ceremonial Honor Guard in Washington, D.C., where he and his crew represented the Coast Guard on a variety of joint service ceremonies throughout the Military District of Washington. He is a career C-130 Hercules pilot who has logged five thousand flight hours with flying assignments at Air Station Elizabeth City (two tours), Air Station Kodiak and the Aviation Repair & Supply Center (ARSC)/Aviation Logistics Center (ALC), which is also in Elizabeth City. ARSC was restructured and renamed ALC during his four-year assignment there. He has enjoyed operational tours flying both the HC-130H Hercules and the newer HC-130J Super Hercules.

In 2017, Eric returned to northeastern North Carolina for a fourth assignment at Base Elizabeth City, where he took command of the HC-27J Asset Project Office (APO). As the APO commanding officer, he and his unit were charged with bringing 14 HC-27J Spartan twin-engine, turbo-prop, fixed-wing aircraft into Coast Guard service. This effort required the regeneration of thirteen of the fourteen aircraft from "the Boneyard" in Tucson, Arizona, where the Department of Defense fleet of C-27J aircraft were placed in long-term storage by the U.S. Air Force. The Coast

Guard's HC-27J Spartan aircraft will serve as replacements for several of the older HC-130H aircraft as they reach the end of their service lives and will augment the fleet of newer HC-130J Super Hercules and HC-144B Ocean Sentry aircraft. Eric has numerous military awards, including two Coast Guard Achievement Medals, one for the *SeaBreeze* rescue and one for a challenging rescue in Alaska. He retired from the Coast Guard in 2020 and is now a civilian maintenance test pilot at the Aviation Logistics Center, and he is dual qualified in the HC-130J and HC-27J aircraft.

Eric is a second-generation Coast Guard man; his father is a 1965 graduate of the Coast Guard Academy and a Coast Guard combat veteran who served as the commanding officer of the U.S. Coast Guard Cutter *Point Cypress* in Vietnam. Eric resides in Chesapeake, Virginia, with his wife of twenty years, Laurie, their two children and two Labrador retrievers.

WHEN I FIRST HAD thoughts of writing about the *SeaBreeze* rescue, I did not have an accurate appreciation for the incredible amount of research it would require. Research was challenging due to the date of the event. In the past twenty years, most of the air crews have retired from the Coast Guard and moved on to other pursuits. The search and rescue records that had been kept by Coast Guard Air Station Elizabeth City had passed their expiration dates and been turned over to the National Archives. The marine weather records that had been kept by the National Weather Service (National Oceanic and Atmospheric Administration) had also been archived but in a different location. Lastly, Coast Guard history, which is so integral to this story, is incredibly voluminous. Luckily, I found some friends in my time of need.

WILLIAM THIESEN, PhD, COAST GUARD HISTORIAN, COAST GUARD ATLANTIC AREA

Bill provided hands-on assistance and direction as to the internal record-keeping process of the Coast Guard. Additionally, he helped identify what information was in the public domain and what was not. Had he not taken the extra step to help in the very early stages of research, I'm not certain that I would have continued to climb the mountain.

George Hall

George Hall, a seasoned photojournalist, covered this rescue for a prominent magazine and published an article in 2001. In researching for this article, he conducted interviews, gathered photographs and other supportive material and had his own plans of writing a book about the *SeaBreeze* rescue. George died in 2006, leaving his wife, Nicky, with a treasure trove of a lifetime's work in photography and journalism. I contacted Nicky, who graciously agreed to help with this project. She provided material that was critical in locating many members of the flight crew.

CWO 4 Michael Christiansen

As part of an overly arduous effort to obtain the Coast Guard's permission to access archived files at the Federal Records Center in Atlanta, I was given incorrect sailing directions and shoaled-up at Christiansen's office at Coast Guard Air Station Elizabeth City. Even though it was out of his AOR, he took the time to give me compass corrections to help ply these uncharted waters. Thank you.

PACM Tom Cowan

Master Chief Cowan and I served together in the Coast Guard Reserve when I was the commanding officer of the Salt Lake City Coast Guard Reserve Unit. Fortunately, for me, we kept in touch through the years. Tom went on to challenging positions in his reserve and civilian career. He served as command master chief for District 11, Maintenance Logistic Command, and Pacific Area & Coast Guard Defense Force West. As a civilian, he was chief of plans, exercises and operations for Joint Force Headquarters in Washington, D.C., and is currently the director of the Air Force Public Affairs Agency's largest and most technologically advanced video production facility located at Hill AFB, Utah. At one point during the research phase of this project, I had extreme difficulty getting quality photographs for the book. I dug into my contacts list to send out a distress call. Tom came to the rescue. He, in turn, elicited the help of longtime friends and colleagues Jeff Smith and Chris Rose at the Coast Guard *Reservist* magazine. Many of the photographs in *On the Wings* came from Tom's special effort to help. I am thankful.

LTJG Ryan Harrigan

Ryan was my liaison with Coast Guard Air Station Elizabeth City. He is a C-130 pilot flying the new J model, and he had the collateral duty of command public affairs officer. For several months, he was just a voice on the phone, working behind the scenes to arrange for interviews, site visits, courtesy calls and, finally, a tour of the Air Station so that I could fully understand the setting. I especially appreciate his follow-up and attention to detail. He is an exemplar of what today's junior officer should be.

Liana Zambresky

Liana is a retired meteorologist who was last working at the Fleet Numerical Meteorology and Oceanography Center in Monterey, California. She is also a neighbor of mine. Wanting to translate the foreign language of weather forecasting to accurately describe (in plain English) the weather conditions encountered by both *SeaBreeze* and Coast Guard aircraft, I asked for help. Hoping to get a synopsis from her after studying the weather reports for that day, her initial response was that the weather "was really, really bad." She explained MUCAPES, deep layer shear and rotating updrafts, all of which I have already forgotten. I thank her for her interest and assistance.

Commander Jim Hadley

Hidden in every person's life story is an inspirational character who contributed much and received little credit for it. After graduating from Coast Guard Officer Candidate School in Virginia and receiving a commission as an ensign, I was assigned to the Thirteenth Coast Guard District in Seattle, Washington. I reported for duty to CDR Hadley, my first commanding officer.

Jim was a "mustang" officer, climbing up the hawse pipe from enlisted ranks to the officer corps. He wasn't just "salty," he had barnacles. On entering his office to "report in," I was not asked to sit, and for the better part of fifteen minutes, he explained to me that ensigns "were not really officers." He summoned Master Chief Boatswain Mate Dan Stack, one of the most senior enlisted in the District, who came into the office and *took a seat*. He told the master chief that he had a new helper and that I would work alongside him; in the process, I was to learn what he would teach. Such a move was incredibly devastating to me as a new ensign, and in the very first day, I contemplated an immediate transfer.

The directive was nothing short of genius. I learned the core values of the Coast Guard's history, protocol, tradition and military bearing from the master chief. I was selected for a promotion to lieutenant junior grade in just twelve months. I was underway at the time, and the commanding officer called to say that it was nice to have a new officer aboard.

I was later selected to be temporary aide to RADM Joseph J. McClelland, the incoming Thirteenth District Commander. Jim knew that junior officers had little extra money, and in fact, I lived paycheck to paycheck. The collateral duty as Admiral's aide required full dress uniforms and a Coast Guard sword. Having no extra money, I borrowed Jim's sword frequently until he finally told me to keep it at home and return it later.

Years passed, and we kept in close communication after his retirement. He called one day to tell me that he drove himself to the hospital and that he was not getting out. I came immediately to help with papers and other uncomfortable arrangements, and on the last day of my visit, he told me from his deathbed to go to the closet in his bedroom and take his sword. It destroyed me emotionally, but I did it. Since then, I have worn that sword in many formal events, and each time I have "buckled up," I have felt a certain presence. I would never have written a book like this without him being in my life—and you can take that to the bank.

OVER SEVENTY PEOPLE CONTRIBUTED to this four-year project. Some deserve special mention: General Ed Eberhart, Vice Admiral Sally Brice O'Hara, Admiral Paul Zukunft, Rear Admiral Brendan McPherson, Rod Ansley, Don Estes, Mark Ward, Dave Neel, Sam Pulliam, Tina Dell'Orco, Lorne Green, Laura Guth, Captain Ben Cooper, Jake Denton, Bruce Nierenberg, LTJG Zachary Georgia, YN2 Claire Burlette, Michael Mc Cleary, Sam Watson (Randy Watson's father) and Rear Admiral Mike Ryan. Many took the time to review draft material to ensure accuracy or otherwise contribute to this project. I thank each one of them for their time and effort and their dedication and devotion to duty in the service of their nation. Semper Par!

Also, special thanks to **MARK BLAZER** at the Federal Records Center in Atlanta, Georgia; **SARA BREWER** at the National Archives at the Atlanta

Regional Office; **WILLIAM BROWN** at the National Climatic Data Center, NOAA; **TAM COMMUNICATIONS** for being a caretaker of so much of the Coast Guard's video archives; **GALEN VARON**; **JON OTTMAN**; as well as **Sandy Johnston** and **Damon Stuebner** of the Alaska State Library.

I feel compelled to mention my wife, **CINDY**. She was the impetus behind starting another book. Fortunately—or unfortunately—she reads too many articles on health, healthy foods, the importance of exercise, disease prevention, blah, blah, blah. One article she read recently had to do with idle minds leading to dementia. Knowing that I had precious little cognitive ability left, she pushed me from the television to the laptop, and for that, I am grateful.

Lastly, and most importantly, there are many other heroes who go without any recognition. Nothing can be said to truly describe the contributions of THE MILITARY SPOUSE, both at home and from afar. Those who have chosen a profession that requires them to act in the most dangerous of times have found mates who fully understand the dangers but also understand what drives those they love to do what they do. Aside from the challenges of frequent moves to new duty stations, raising a family and being both a lover and a friend, they live with the uncertainty of tomorrow more than most. The military spouse is truly the staysail of the family ship, calming the effects of heavy weather and providing subtle assistance in keeping to the charted course.

> *I wasn't too many miles into a voyage from Costa Rica to the Galapagos onboard a Jim Brown Searunner trimaran before I'd fallen in love with our staysail. It was our first line of defense in heavy weather, providing just the right amount of sail area and maintaining the same center of effort or "leverage point" under a double-reefed main as we had with the full rig. It was a trouble-free sail to backwind when we were heaving-to in moderate winds or needed a push coming about, or help getting on the right tack when sailing off the anchor.*[46]

So, to the spouses who wait up at night for your loved ones to return, this book is really about you, too. You chose to be with someone who wears the cloth of our nation, and for that, we are grateful.

IN MEMORIAM

LCDR Randall Edward Watson, USCG Ret.

R andy Watson, aged fifty-seven, passed away suddenly on January 17, 2018, in Fremont, California. He was born at Barksdale Air Force Base, Louisiana, in 1960. He graduated from Georgia Southern University in 1983 and was commissioned in the U.S. Army at Fort Bragg, North Carolina. Randy completed rotary wing pilot training at Fort Rucker, Alabama, in 1984 and was assigned to the 101st Airborne Division at Fort Campbell, Kentucky. After a tour in South Korea in 1989, he was assigned to Fort Hood, Texas. In 1991, he transferred to the U.S. Coast Guard and was stationed at Air Station Elizabeth City, North Carolina. Following a tour at Air Station Kodiak, Alaska, and a second tour at Elizabeth City, he retired from the Coast Guard in 2003 and was employed as a test pilot and aircraft manager for the U.S. Army at Moffett Field, California, until 2017.

Randy received several awards for rescue missions while in the Coast Guard, including the Distinguished Flying Cross and four Air Medals. In 1994, Randy was a member of the Coast Guard crew that received the Naval Helicopter Association Aircrew of the Year Award. In 2001, Randy and other aircrew members from Air Station Elizabeth City received the Frederick L. Feinberg Memorial Award from the American Helicopter Society (AHS) International for their part in rescuing thirty-four crewmen from the *SeaBreeze*. Randy logged over 5,100 flight hours while on active duty.

LCDR Randy Watson in front of the helicopter he flew in the *SeaBreeze* rescue mission. *Photograph courtesy of Sam Watson.*

GLOSSARY

AET. Aviation Electronics Technician.

AFCS. Automatic flight control system.

AMT (AMT2). Aviation Maintenance Technician (Aviation Maintenance Technician Second Class).

AMVER. Automated mutual assistance vessel rescue system, a maritime mutual assistance system to aid search and rescue operations.

ANG. Air National Guard.

Angels. A military term (most often used in the Navy) for rescue helicopters.

AOR. Area of responsibility.

AST. Aviation Survival Technician.

AVT. In 2003, the AVT rating was re-designated as AET, Avionics Electronics Technician.

CAPT. Captain.

CDR. Commander.

channel 16. The international maritime distress frequency of 156.8 MHz, VHF-FM.

COMSAT. A commercial satellite communications company serving mariners, among others.

contingency power. Most helicopter turbine engines are rated for a maximum continuous power, which does not have a time constraint. As the term implies, contingency power allows engines to temporarily provide additional power beyond the maximum-rated continuous power. This is done by electronically raising the temperature limiter on the engine, and as the hotter turbine engine air/fuel mixture burns, more power is produced. However, this power can only be used on a time-limited basis without engine damage or failure. More power produced by the engines translates to more thrust produced by the rotor system, as the engines are driving the rotors through the main transmission.

D5. Fifth Coast Guard District with offices in Portsmouth, Virginia.

ENS. Ensign.

H-3F. A Sikorsky amphibious helicopter or Pelican.

H-60. Sikorsky helicopter with service variants Black Hawk, Pave, Jayhawk.

HC-130. A fixed-wing, four-engine, turboprop cargo plane.

HF. High-frequency radio communications band.

HMS. Her Majesty's ship.

KT. Knot, a measure of speed. One knot is equal to 1.15 statute miles per hour.

LANTAREA. Coast Guard Atlantic Area, a parent command to the Fifth Coast Guard District and others. Atlantic Area offices are located in Portsmouth, Virginia.

LCDR. Lieutenant Commander.

LT. Lieutenant.

LTJG. Lieutenant Junior Grade.

M/V. Motor vessel.

NAS. Naval Air Station.

NM. Nautical mile. One nautical mile is 6,067 feet or 1.15 statute miles.

ODO. Operations Duty Officer.

OPCEN. Operations Center.

OPTEMPO. Operations tempo.

OSC. On-scene Commander.

RCC. Rescue Coordination Center.

RMS. Royal Mail Steamer.

RTB. Return to base.

S/V. Sailing vessel.

SAR HELOS. Search and rescue helicopters.

SAR. Search and rescue.

SITREP. Situation report.

TACAN. Tactical air navigation system, which is used by military aircraft to determine range and bearing to another station or aircraft.

TCAS. Traffic collision avoidance system, which provides warning to pilots to prevent midair collisions with other aircraft.

thunderstorm lights. Internal lighting to illuminate the cockpit when flying in storm-darkened skies.

translational lift. Translational lift/effective translational lift (ETL). Helicopter rotor systems are more efficient in forward flight versus hovering. In a hover, rotor tip vortices recirculate through the rotor system, causing turbulence and resulting in a need for additional power. But in forward flight, the vortices and turbulence experienced in hovering flight are left behind as the air flow becomes more horizontal. This accounts for the increased efficiency of the rotor system in forward flight over hovering. While transitioning to forward flight, the actual point at which the helicopter finally outruns the vortices and turbulence to achieve efficiency is known as effective translational lift (ETL) and occurs around sixteen to twenty-four knots.

UHF. Ultra-high frequency.

USCG. United States Coast Guard.

VADM. Vice Admiral (three-star admiral).

VHF-FM. Very high frequency—frequency modulation, a line-of-sight radio band commonly used by mariners. The international maritime distress frequency is 156.8 MHz, VHF-FM.

weak link. The link connecting the trail line to the connection on the rescue basket. This link is designed to break at a given load to prevent an entangled trail line from tethering the helicopter to a vessel or fixed object.

NOTES

Preface

1. President George W. Bush, "Hurricane Katrina: Lessons Learned—Chapter Four: A Week of Crisis (August 29–September 5)," September 15, 2005, www.georgewbush-whitehouse.archives.gov.

Chapter 1

2. U.S. Coast Guard History Program, "Bear, 1885," www.media.defense.gov.
3. National Park Service, "U.S. Life-Saving Service," www.nps.gov.
4. *Coast Guard Compass*, "Coast Guard Heroes Kathleen Moore," November 5, 2010, www.compass.coastguard.blog.
5. Stu Beitler, "Nantucket, MA Lightship *NANTUCKET* Sunk, May 1934," *Winnipeg Free Press* (Manitoba), May 16, 1934, www.gendisasters.com.
6. U.S. Coast Guard, "U.S. Coast Guard Facts," Boating, www.uscgboating.org.

Chapter 2

7. "Pigeons Helping Coast Guard Find Victims at Sea," *Hour*, July 15, 1982, www.news.google.com.
8. U.S. Coast Guard, "Air Cushion Vehicle," Coast Guard Historian's Office, www.history.uscg.mil.

9. U.S. Coast Guard, "Unmanned Aircraft Systems," Coast Guard Historian's Office, www.history.uscg.mil.

10. U.S. Coast Guard, "Grumman UF-1G/2G (later HU-16E) 'Albatross' or 'Goat,'" Coast Guard Historian's Office, www.history.uscg.mil.

11. U.S. Coast Guard, "U.S. Coast Guard Rescue Swimmer Program," Coast Guard Historian's Office, www.history.uscg.mil.

Chapter 3

12. U.S. Coast Guard, "Significant Dates in Coast Guard Aviation," U.S. Coast Guard Historian's Office, www.history.uscg.mil.

Chapter 4

13. National Park Service, "Kitty Hawk," www.nps.gov.

14. David Weydert, "Coast Guardsmen Pioneered Flight with Wright Brothers," *Maritime Executive*, December 17, 2014.

15. White House of President Barack Obama, "Presidential Proclamation—Wright Brothers Day, 2015," Office of the Press Secretary, www.whitehouse.gov.

Chapter 5

16. Air Station Elizabeth City Wardroom, *Coast Guard Base Elizabeth City* (Charleston, SC: Arcadia Publishing, 2005).

17. William H. Thiesen, "The History of the 'Racing Stripe' Emblem and Brand, Part I: The United States Coast Guard," *Sea History* 139 (Summer 2012): 28–33, www.media.defense.gov.

18. Notable VMI graduates include General George Marshall, General of the Army, Secretary of War, Secretary of State, author the Marshall European Recovery Plan (for which he received the Nobel Peace Prize) and, later, the president of the American Red Cross; General Shepperd, Commandant of the Marine Corps; and General Johnny Jumper, who served as Air Force Chief of Staff. Mathew Fontaine Maury and General "Stone Wall" Jackson were both instructors at VMI.

Chapter 7

19. PACS Carolyn Cihelka, "U.S. Coast Guard Media Advisory," December 22, 1999.
20. Katie Braynard, "Remembering Munro," *Coast Guard Compass*, September 27, 2015, www.coastguard.dodlive.mil.
21. Coast Guard Cutter *Pontchartrain* had a single five-inch 38-caliber deck gun. The gun could fire "star shells," sometimes called "starburst shells," which were designed to provide illumination of the night sky.
22. Reprinted courtesy of the Pan Am Historical Foundation. Coastguardsman Ronald Christian left the rescue boat and entered the sinking forward section of the aircraft to search for remaining passengers.
23. Christopher Lagan, "History Arctic Rescue Changes Face of Coast Guard Operations," *Coast Guard Compass*, www.coastguard.dodlive.mil.
24. Galen Varon, "Rescue of the *Alaskan Monarch*," *American Queen*, March 14, 2012, www.thecutterstoris.weebly.com.
25. Coast Guard Aviation Association, "1995—Migrant Interdiction-Operation ABLE RESPONSE and Beyond," www.cgaviationhistory.org.
26. CPO William Epperson, "U.S. Coast Guard Media Advisory," December 27, 2000.

Chapter 8

27. Reprinted with permission from Captain James Lowe, www.Caribbean-Pirates.com.
28. University of Arizona Library, USS *Arizona* Collection.

Chapter 9

29. Jake Denton, "The Greatest Rescue," *Virginia Living*, December 2006.
30. Ibid.

Chapter 10

31. Jason D. Neubauer, "Steam Ship *El Faro* (O.N. 561732) Sinking and Loss of the Vessel with 33 Persons Missing and Presumed Deceased Northeast

of Acklins and Crooked Island, Bahamas on October 1, 2015, Marine Board's Report," U.S. Department of Homeland Security, U.S. Coast Guard, September 24, 2017, www.media.defense.gov.

32. National Transportation Safety Board, "Safety Recommendation Report: Tropical Cyclone Information for Mariners," October 1, 2015, www.iho.int.

33. International Maritime Organization, "Maritime Safety," www.imo.org.

34. National Oceanic and Atmospheric Administration, "Our History: NOAA's Roots Reach Back More than 200 Years: We are America's Environmental Intelligence Agency," www.noaa.gov.

35. Nathaniel Bowditch, *The American Practical Navigator 2002 Bicentennial Edition* (Springfield, VA: National Geospatial-Intelligence Agency, 2002), 613.

36. National Oceanic and Atmospheric Administration, "United States Coast Pilot®," www.nauticalcharts.noaa.gov.

Chapter 11

37. With the failure of the TCAS, CG 1504 was left with no radar capability to maintain separation of multiple aircraft. TACAN (tactical air navigation system) only allowed distance tracking for one of five aircraft flying the mission at a time.

38. ICS is the internal communication system, which allows flight crew members to talk to each other through their headsets or helmets.

39. A weak link is designed into the top of the trail line to break at three hundred pounds of stress. This prevents the helicopter from becoming tethered to the vessel in the event that the trail line becomes entangled with the vessel's rigging.

40. Wallops Flight Facility is operated by NASA and is located on the eastern shore of Virginia, approximately one hundred miles north-northeast of Norfolk on the peninsula between Delaware Bay and Chesapeake Bay. In addition to fuel availability, it provides crash, fire and rescue services.

Chapter 12

41. Because this meeting was hastily called, LT Molthen was not prepared to address the implication that the helicopter was "overloaded" in terms of

weight that the helicopter could safely hold, given the amount of fuel that had already burned in flying over 235 nautical miles getting to *SeaBreeze*. This is discussed in a subsequent chapter.

Chapter 14

42. Captain G. Russell, "Coast Guard Aviators and Another Daring Rescue," *Bulletin*, February 2001. Reprinted courtesy of Coast Guard Academy Alumni Association.
43. "Coast Guard Operations," *Sikorsky News*, May 15, 2001.
44. The HH-60J Jayhawk is also equipped with an external cargo hook with a rated capacity of six thousand pounds.
45. Petty Officer Third Class Nicole Foguth, "Raising the Bar in a Single Hoist," *Coast Guard Compass*, May 16, 2018, www.coastguard.dodlive.mil.

Acknowledgements

46. Reprinted courtesy of Carol Hasse, Hasse and Company, Port Townsend Sails.

ABOUT THE AUTHOR

Rear Admiral Moore served in the United States Coast Guard, both active and reserve, for over thirty years. In response to the events of 9/11, he served as Deputy Commander, Coast Guard Atlantic Area. He had temporary duty overseas on six occasions, including in Japan, Bahrain and Germany. He was awarded the Legion of Merit and Coast Guard Distinguished Service Medal, among other honors. In civilian employment, Governor Schwarzenegger appointed him as Administrator, California Office of Spill Prevention and Response, and he was responsible for a comprehensive environmental protection and response organization. He administered various maritime programs at the state level, affecting the shipping industry, maritime towing companies and port authorities, and he responded to oil spills and other leaks of hazardous materials on state and federal waters. Previous to that, he was Special Legal Counsel to the Administrator. He is a member of the California State Bar. He is the ex-President of the Sacramento chapter of the Navy League and served as vice president of the Sacramento Optimist Club, supporting programs for disadvantaged youth. He and his wife, Cindy, are retired and living near Lake Tahoe in Northern California.